RACHEL HARDAGE BARRETT is the editor-in-chief of *Country Living*. A Tennessee native, she takes her tea half sweet, collects Kentucky Derby glassware, and someday hopes to retire to a Low-Country farmhouse with a big live oak out front. She lives in Birmingham, Alabama, with her family, but still makes it to Neyland Stadium at least once a year.

JEANNE LYONS DAVIS grew up in Louisiana where she cultivated her weakness for wicker furniture, penchant for estate sales and palate for plate lunches. She has been an editor at *Country Living* and *Southern Living* and contributor for *Architectural Digest*, *Atlanta Homes & Lifestyles*, *Brides*, and *Coastal Living*. She lives in Louisiana with her tenacious kids and dog of dubious origins.

The SOUTHERNER'S
Y'ALLMANAC

The SOUTHERNER'S
Y'ALLMANAC

HEARST HOME

CONTENTS

Spring
PAGE 11

Summer
PAGE 63

Fall
PAGE 117

Because we're not good at winter.

Holidays
PAGE 171

WELCOME, Y'ALL

❖

Y'all. Is there a more wonderfully inclusive word in the English language? I recently ran across a study—a collaborative endeavor between the University of Georgia and Georgia Tech—that says the Southern accent is fading. This, of course, comes as no surprise. Technology—social media, in particular—has transformed the world we live in, and, unlike previous generations that mostly exchanged banter on the porch, our world is far less insular and therefore shaped by a broader-reaching set of influences. In many ways, that's a good thing. The more connected we are, perhaps the more open-minded and empathetic we can be. (Or so we can hope.) But, even if the Southern accent fades, I'm optimistic that the region will maintain a certain magic that doesn't exist anywhere else.

I grew up in North Carolina and Tennessee, and I've spent most of my adult life split between New York City and Birmingham, Alabama, and I can tell you this: The South is special. It's apparent in my neighborhood text chain. ("Who wants to have drinks on my porch tonight?" "Anyone need extra tomatoes?") I see it in the casserole-scheduling frenzy for friends in need. Granted, it's not perfect—that's another book unto itself—but I find folks down here view the region as they would a wayward but well-meaning relative: complicated and flawed but worth loving with all your might.

This book is a celebration of the unique charms of the region, none of which are rooted in linguistics. (Okay, there may be just *a few* beloved Southern expressions in these pages.) You'll find ways to porch (yes, it's a verb) throughout every season, ideas for showcasing Southern hospitality (so many centerpieces and place settings!), gorgeous gardens, and recipes that serve up familiar favorites in fresh ways (Cheerwine Ribs! Hummingbird Bundt Cake!). I should also acknowledge that there are certain things Southerners cannot fully lay claim to as a culture (mason jars, fireflies, college football), but—because they're as clung to our consciousness as kudzu to the landscape—they felt worthy of inclusion. So, while our accents may fade, our Southernness isn't going anywhere. Because *y'all* isn't just a word—it's a way of life.

—RACHEL HARDAGE BARRETT

GILCHRIST
SINCE 1928
STILL A MTN BROOK
TRADITION

CORNED BEEF & SWISS
OR
REUBEN STYLE
SANDWICH
2.99

DRINKS
LIME ADE - OUR SPECIALTY
GRAPE   CHERRY
SM 2.29 LG 2.89 X LG 2.99
GALLON OF LIME ADE 15.99
FOUNTAIN & BOTTLE DRINKS
COFFEE
TEA
HOT CHOC
ICE 20 30 40

PLATES
CHICKEN
TUNA   SALAD   7.25
HAM   EACH
EGG
PIMENTO
ADDITIONAL SCOOPS 4.25
ASPIC
COTTAGE CHEESE   EA H 3.25
POTATO SALAD

SALADS BY THE OUNCE
8 OZ   7.85   TAKE OUT
16   10.85   ONLY

SOUPS
CHIC NOODLE
                  CUP   BOWL
TOMATO   3.25   4.25

SEASONAL
HOME MADE CHILI
        CUP   BOWL
        4.75   5.75

ICE CREAM GOODIES
SHAKES & MALTS   5.00
CHOC - STRAW - VAN   EACH
OLD FASHIONED SODAS
ICE CREAM FLOATS

SINGLE DIP   2.90
CONE OR BOWL

BREAKFAST
PLAIN BISCUIT OR TOAST 1.50
BAC - SAU - HAM BISCUIT 2.50
EGG BISCUIT   2.90
ADD MEAT   3.69
ADD CHEESE   .40
EGG PLATE   4.25
BAGEL WITH CREAM CHEESE 2.96

Enjoying a beverage at Gilchrist, a soda fountain in Birmingham, Alabama. (See page 110 for more spots to sip and stay awhile.)

INTRODUCTION

For more than 200 years, *The Old Farmer's Almanac* has been a trusted resource of tips, tricks, and helpful tactics for farmers and gardeners to reference and rely on through the changing seasons. Down here in the South, we, too, are extremely attuned to the seasons (garden-party season, peach season, football season...), which is why we decided to create our own handbook of sorts—one that acts as both a practical and an inspirational year-round reference, while simultaneously shining a spotlight on our iconic idiosyncrasies.

Like *The Old Farmer's Almanac, The Southerner's Y'allmanac* is organized by seasons, but, in addition to advice of the pragmatic kind (how to grow azaleas, the best way to polish silver, the art of a thank-you note), you'll also find plenty of beautiful imagery (inviting interiors! must-try recipes! striking centerpieces!), as well as quirky tidbits and Southern I-never-knew-thats. (For example, did you know cotton candy was invented by a Nashville dentist, or that a single Kentucky Derby glass from the 1930s is worth up to $5,000?)

Throughout these pages, you'll also enjoy wit and wisdom from a few notable Southerners—chefs, gardeners, designers, shop owners, musicians— who contribute to the diverse melting pot (or shall we say rich and flavorful gumbo?) of the modern American South. Whether you're a native Southerner or a Southerner in spirit, we hope these pages capture the convivial atmosphere of the region that turned tailgating into an art form and made porching a pastime. And if they don't, well, bless your heart.

SO, WHERE IS "THE SOUTH," ANYWAY?

Well, that depends on whom you ask. Traditionally, the South consists of these states:

- **Alabama**
- **Arkansas**
- **Delaware (yes, really!)**
- **Florida**
- **Georgia**
- **Kentucky**
- **Louisiana**
- **Maryland (yep)**
- **Mississippi**
- **North Carolina**
- **Oklahoma**
- **South Carolina**
- **Tennessee**
- **Texas**
- **Virginia**
- **West Virginia**

While the Mid-Atlantic states have carved out their own cultural identity (see: crab cakes! lacrosse!), there are other states beyond this sweet 16 (lookin' at you, **Missouri**) that boast accents and cultural commonalities that give them the honorary designation.

Still, Southern is a state of mind. Biscuits and bourbon, after all, know no boundaries.

WISHFUL THINKING

Roughly 85 percent of spring dandelion wishes relate to the upcoming college football season.

Spring

It's Not *Spring* in the South Without...

·····◇·····

The intoxicating scent of
honeysuckle and star jasmine
mixed with laundry on the line

◇

Forcing the whole family
to begrudgingly pose in front
of the azalea bushes

◇

Finding any excuse to twirl up
the table with floral china

◇

Fresh strawberries from
the U-pick farm, followed by
strawberry shortcake,
strawberry pie, strawberry-
pretzel salad...

◇

Dyeing Easter eggs before
watching *Steel Magnolias* for
the umpteenth time

◇

Heading to horse country
in your finest wide-brimmed
hat or seersucker blazer

◇

Shelling peas on the porch
into a colander on your lap

◇

Doing your best to bypass
spring break traffic along the
back roads (while counting
every cow on the way)

· SPRING ·

Around the House

---◇---

"In my opinion, what sets a home apart is when you focus on your family's story rather than a style ideal. Find pieces that speak to you, and give yourself the freedom to tell your story in your own unique way."

—Television personality and longtime Texan Joanna Gaines

Rocking chairs required.

The Southern Checklist

Create a Party-Ready Porch

····◇····

Refresh Your Linen Closet

····◇····

Try a Skirted Table

If it was good enough for William Faulkner...

····◇····

Embrace a Hue with History

····◇····

Somewhere, Grandma is smiling.

Add Charm with Chintz

Design a Party-Ready Porch

I f the kitchen is the heart of a Southern home, the porch is its soul. And come spring, the soul stirs with anticipation—of warmer temperatures, of pulling out the seersucker, of glasses clink-clink-clinking into the blissfully balmy wee hours. While the dog days of summer may call for afternoon porch naps and general lazing about, spring is the time to emerge from winter hibernation in the name of neighborly congregation. So, go ahead and shuffle that deck of cards, cue up a playlist (see page 60), and bring out the bourbon as you transition your favorite space into party mode.

Take note: There are no hard-and-fast rules when it comes to the art of porching. That would be incongruous with the very idea, so just consider these polite suggestions.

NO. 1

Help-Yourself Hutch

Lighten your hosting load by keeping commonly requested items (napkins, bottle openers) within reach.

NO. 2

Conversation Stations

Offer guests multiple spots to sit a spell as opposed to gathering at one table—it'll make for more casual mingling.

NO. 3

Lantern Lighting

For extra ambience come dusk, fill mason jars with battery-operated tea lights and string them from the ceiling.

NO. 4

Wheelbarrow Bar Cart

Let the good times roll—and set a casual tone—by filling the backyard staple with ice and beverages.

ICED TEA

Some say tea is like moonshine—as in, if you don't make it yourself, it's not the real deal. For a proper home-brewed pitcher, bring 4 cups of **water** to a boil in a small saucepan, then remove from heat. Add 3 family-size or 12 individual **tea bags** (Lipton or Luzianne is usually the go-to) and leave submerged for 5 minutes, then discard. Add 1 cup **granulated sugar*** and stir until dissolved. Pour into a pitcher, followed by 3 quarts of water to make a gallon. Refrigerate 4 hours. Serve over **ice** and add a **slice of lemon,** if desired.

*You may need to add more if you're from the Deep South or have a double name.

ALL IN A NAME
Bella, Max, and Charlie top the list of Southern dog names. (For something a bit more novel, try Delta, Whiskey, or Waylon.)

Refresh Your Linen Closet

Leontine Linens founder **Jane Scott Hodges** on the art of personalization

"I believe everyone loves an opportunity to 'make their mark,' and what better way than a monogram, with seemingly endless color palette options and opportunities to play with scale and style. We are near our 50,000th order, and the Etienne monogram, one of the first I introduced, is still by far one of my favorites because it's timeless and ornamental without being fussy or overly ornate. For lasting linens, I love suggesting ivory napkins with a soft gold monogram. It's the little black dress of the table because it magically works with every china pattern and place setting. While monogramming etiquette continues to evolve with modern interpretations (combining two last names), it's important to remember that there is no wrong way to create a monogram that is meaningful to you and your family."

Having a dedicated space to organize your linens gives you a better opportunity to actually use them in your daily life," says Jane Scott Hodges, founder of Leontine Linens, who has integrated several "linen closets" throughout her New Orleans home (including the armoire-turned-closet above). "Linen storage boards are also a game changer when it comes to stacking sets." Liz Eichholz, cofounder and creative director of Southern-based luxury towel company Weezie, says the company sees a significant spike in sales each spring. High-quality towels have a shelf life of about two years, so if it's time to restock, consider a monogram or, as Liz suggests, an embroidered nod to geography (a zip code) or cheeky phrase (for example, powder room hand towels that say "Please leave by 9").

TRY A SKIRTED TABLE

·······················

No. 1
IN THE ENTRY
A blue-and-white skirt topped with ginger jars and coffee-table books adds up to a graceful entrance.

No. 2
IN A SUNROOM
In Birmingham, Alabama, a trellis motif feels in keeping with wicker chairs and garden-ready accessories.

No. 3
IN THE LIVING ROOM
A fringed skirt brings refinement to a rustic North Carolina cabin by designer Whitney McGregor.

No. 4
IN A KITCHEN
Stripes add softness to a sunny breakfast room styled by Mississippi native Page Mullins.

EMBRACE A HUE WITH HISTORY

For a brush with greatness, look to these paint picks that
passed muster with some of the region's more notable people and places.

RANDOLPH BLUE
Benjamin Moore

Colonial Williamsburg
historians developed this
shade based on pigments
from 18th-century wallpaper
found in the colony.

WILLOW
Fine Paints of Europe

George Washington enjoyed
this verdant hue on the
walls of the New Room in
Mount Vernon, his
fabled Virginia farmhouse.

CAMEO AZALEA
Fine Paints of Europe

The ballroom of
West Virginia's storied
Greenbrier Resort
features this punchy,
party-ready hue.

SWEET SHERRY
Pratt & Lambert

Influenced by Creole and
Caribbean cultures, this
peachy pink spans the exterior
of homes in New Orleans
and other coastal cities.

GALAPAGOS GREEN
Pantone

The verdant hue is
seen on the shutters of
William Faulkner's
Rowan Oak home in
Oxford, Mississippi.

GOLDEN BISCUIT
Valspar

This buttery shade is
slathered on the
kitchen walls of Laura
Ingalls Wilder's home in
southern Missouri.

A SHORT HISTORY OF...

Haint Blue

This watery blue porch-ceiling staple can be traced to the Gullah
Geechee community of the Low Country (descendants of Africans who
were enslaved on the plantations of the lower Atlantic coast). They
painted this blue-green shade on ceilings to prevent evil spirits,
called "haints," from haunting them at night. (It was thought to mimic
the look of water, which ghosts can't cross). These days, the color
is embraced throughout the South; some claim it wards off wasps.

WATERY
Sherwin-Williams

Add Charm with Chintz

More Chintzpiration

These iconic patterns can be seen in many a Southern home.

Bowood by Colefax & Fowler
This neat repeat was inspired by a swatch of 19th-century fabric uncovered at England's famed Bowood estate.

Pyne Hollyhock by Schumacher
This fabric was famously used by Southern designer Albert Hadley in the 1960s home of New York socialite Nancy Pyne (thus its name).

Floral Bouquet by Lee Jofa
This timeless textile was a favorite of designer Mario Buatta, aka "the Prince of Chintz."

While technically a glazed cotton fabric (hence its subtle sheen), the term *chintz* is now used to reference over-the-top florals of all garden varieties (even wallcoverings, above). And while chintz has never truly fallen out of favor with color-loving, tradition-minded Southerners—just look to Virginia-born design icon Nancy Lancaster or West Virginia's famously floral Greenbrier resort, which has its own line of fabric—it is in full bloom with a new generation who crave bold color and club chair comfort over reserved neutrals and clean lines. "I love oversize blooms—the bolder the better—or unexpected color combos to keep it from feeling fussy," says singer, songwriter, and Southern tastemaker Holly Audrey Williams.

· SPRING ·

At the Table

◆

"What I love about the South is that there is nothing too insignificant to celebrate, and if you're really lucky, you learn about grace and small joys, which are, after all, what make up big lives."
—Author and Mississippi native Julia Reed

The Southern Checklist

Set a Southern Picnic Table

Chambray all day, as they say.

·····◆·····

Pick Your Place Setting

Your Easter table has never looked so good.

·····◆·····

Arrange a Seasonal Centerpiece

·····◆·····

Host the Definitive Derby Party

The higher the hat, the closer to God.

Set a Southern Picnic Table

T here are, of course, picnics of the paper-plate and plastic-utensil variety. But Southerners tend to take things up a notch. Case in point: this pretty pastoral *pique-nique* (that would be French for "picnic") hosted by Texas-born designer Lela Rose, which embraces vintage embossed ceramic plates and down-to-earth chambray linens, as well as the season's floral fanfare in full petal-to-the-metal fashion. "That's the great thing about entertaining outdoors," says Lela. "All of the beauty comes prepackaged with the season. I honestly don't know what I'd do if I were allergic to pollen."

NO. 1
Colorful Wildflowers

A fresh-picked assortment of sweet peas, chamomile, and ranunculus makes the most of the surroundings.

NO. 3
Daisy Dishware

Vintage plates with a bracelet-like border and embroidered napkins lend more wildflower-themed whimsy.

NO. 2
Hoop Place Cards

Thin floral wire secures blooms and name tags to three-inch embroidery hoops.

NO. 4
Shipping Pallet Perch

Constructed from pallets and two-by-fours, the 20-inch-high "table" keeps things low but comfortable.

PICK YOUR PLACE SETTING

·····································

No. 1
WOODLAND WHIMSY
A monogrammed egg
nestled in moss atop
a plate on a round wood
"charger" makes for a
rustic presentation.

No. 2
GARDEN VARIETY
A vintage seed packet
can act as a pretty
sleeve for either a
napkin, flower stem, or
seasonal produce.

No. 3
BLOOM SERVICE
Filled with pretty
pastels and a stenciled
napkin, a dogwood-
themed setting brings
the outdoors in.

No. 4
ALL EARS
Vintage brass bunnies
bring quirky and
collected charm to
this hare-raiser of
a get-together.

Arrange a
Seasonal Centerpiece

If centerpiece-ing were a competitive sport, Southerners
would have the trophy on lock. For Easter, an assortment
of lilacs, anemones, scabiosa lavender, alliums, and
ranunculus is placed in a water-filled glass vase that's nestled
in a vintage wire basket and surrounded by dyed
(or, if preferred, painted wooden) eggs.

HUNT & GATHER
*The Guinness World
Record for the
largest egg hunt goes to
Florida's Cypress
Gardens Adventure Park,
which included
501,000 eggs.*

Host the Definitive Derby Party

Aside from perhaps a private suite at Churchill Downs, there's no
better way to toast the first Saturday of May. And because the main event's
only two minutes long, that leaves more time for eating,
drinking, betting, and belting out the words to "My Old Kentucky Home."

PRIZE PICKS
This two-handled style of trophy is often referred to as a "loving cup," which was used for celebratory drinking at weddings and banquets.

Kentucky Benedictine Dip

Invented by Louisville caterer and tearoom-owner Jennie Carter Benedict, this cream cheese–cucumber dip is a century-old Kentucky classic.

WORKING TIME *15 minutes*
TOTAL TIME *15 minutes*
MAKES *1½ cups*

- 1 **(8-ounce) package cream cheese,** at room temperature
- 1 **small English cucumber (about 8 ounces),** peeled, halved, seeds removed, and roughly chopped
- ⅓ cup **fresh dill,** plus more for garnish
- 2 **scallions,** coarsely chopped
- 2 tablespoons **fresh lemon juice**
- 2 tablespoons **mayonnaise**
- **Kosher salt** and **freshly ground black pepper**
- **Carrot** and **celery sticks,** sliced **bell pepper, radishes,** and **crostini,** for serving

1. Process cream cheese, cucumber, dill, scallions, lemon juice, and mayonnaise in a food processor until smooth. Season with salt and pepper. Transfer to a serving bowl and garnish with fresh dill.

2. Serve with carrot and celery sticks, bell pepper, radishes, and crostini alongside.

Bourbon Derby Punch

Take note: All bourbon is considered whiskey, but not all whiskey is considered bourbon. For a proper Derby party, bourbon is a nonnegotiable.

In a punch bowl or pitcher, combine 2 cups **bourbon,** 1½ cups **club soda,** 1½ cups **orange curaçao** or triple sec, 1 cup **sweet vermouth,** ½ to ¾ cup **fresh lime juice,** and 1 tablespoon **orange bitters.** Serve over ice and garnish with **lime wedges** and **fresh mint.** *Makes six 1-cup servings.*

A SHORT HISTORY OF...

Derby Glassware

In 1938, the Kentucky Derby had decorative glasses made for the Churchill Downs dining hall, but the track's management noticed that people were pocketing them as souvenirs. In 1939, they started producing glasses for profit. These days, they're highly collectible. For example, the circa-1939 sippers at left can now fetch as much as $5,000 each!

SWEET TRADITION
Featuring homemade caramel, melted chocolate, and walnuts, these butter cookies take inspiration from the famed Derby Pie at Kern's Kitchen in Louisville (or Loo-a-vull, as the locals say).

Derby-Inspired Thumbprint Cookies

WORKING TIME *40 minutes* **TOTAL TIME** *1 hour (includes chilling)*
MAKES *about 28 cookies*

2½ **cups all-purpose flour, spooned and leveled, plus more for working**

½ **teaspoon baking powder**

1½ **teaspoons kosher salt, divided**

1 **cup (2 sticks), plus 1 tablespoon unsalted butter at room temperature, divided**

1¾ **cups sugar, divided**

1 **large egg yolk**

1 **teaspoon pure vanilla extract**

⅓ **cup heavy cream**

2 **tablespoons bourbon**

½ **cup chopped toasted walnuts**

½ **cup semisweet chocolate chips**

1. Preheat oven to 350°F. Line two baking sheets with parchment paper. Whisk together flour, baking powder, and ½ teaspoon salt in a bowl.

2. Beat 1 cup butter and ¾ cup sugar with an electric mixer on medium speed until light and fluffy, 1 to 2 minutes. Add egg yolk and vanilla and beat until combined. Reduce mixer speed to low and gradually beat in flour mixture just until combined.

3. Roll heaping tablespoonfuls of dough into balls and place on prepared baking sheets, spacing 2 inches apart. Press a floured ½ teaspoon measuring spoon into each cookie to make a thumbprint. Chill 30 minutes.

4. Bake until golden brown, 16 to 19 minutes. Use ½ teaspoon measuring spoon to reshape thumbprints. Cool on a wire rack.

5. Combine ¼ cup water and remaining 1 cup sugar in a medium saucepan. Cook over medium-low heat, stirring, until sugar has dissolved, 3 to 4 minutes. Stop stirring and cook until deep golden brown, 10 to 12 minutes. Remove from heat and carefully stir in cream and bourbon. Add remaining 1 teaspoon salt and 1 tablespoon butter; swirl until dissolved, let stand 5 minutes. Stir in walnuts and chocolate chips until melted. Let stand 10 minutes. Fill thumbprints with caramel mixture, dividing evenly.

Ask a Southerner
HOW TO STYLE SEERSUCKER

Designer **Sid Mashburn** on the merits of the menswear mainstay

"I look at my seersucker blazer—I don't even own the pants!—as the warm-weather version of my navy blazer. Seersucker was literally invented for the heat in India in the 1600s. It's kind of corrugated, so it never goes flat to your skin, which helps with airflow. It has a lot of range—it's great with jeans, khakis, canvas, linen, wool—and looks just as good with a shirt and tie as it does with a polo. So, you can make it casual and almost beatnik or dressy and elegant. My one rule of thumb is that I don't usually wear patterns with it (except neckwear), so I would just eliminate any patterned shirts. And then I would lean into oxfords (the fabric gives it some ease) in almost any color, chambray, or polos. And you don't want to do the white bucks with the seersucker; it's a little too on the nose, particularly if you live someplace that isn't the South, you run the risk of looking straight out of Central Casting."

In the Garden

"All gardens need time, and part of the great pleasure of gardening, it seems to me, is watching them mature."
—Author and Virginia native Bunny Williams

The Southern Checklist

Spruce Up the Potting Shed

⸻ ◇ ⸻

Stop and Smell the Azaleas

...and more spring flowers we love!

⸻ ◇ ⸻

Perfect the Porch Planter

Three words: thriller, filler, and spiller.

⸻ ◇ ⸻

Display Your Dogwoods

You knew the ol' man's fishing creel would come in handy someday.

LOTTA 'COTTA
An antique bottle-drying rack can be used to hold an assortment of pots. For a decorative touch, place a wide container on top and fill with plants.

SPRUCE UP THE POTTING SHED

....

No. 1
RUSTIC RACK
The ever-versatile
shipping pallet comes
in handy as a wall
organizer for odds
and ends.

No. 2
HOOK HELPER
Twine remains at the
ready courtesy of
a single hardworking
butcher's hook.
(Just slip it over a slat—
no nail required.)

No. 3
REPURPOSED RAKE
When facing
outward, the toothed
bar of a bow rake
can be used to hang
and corral tools.

No. 4
CLEVER CADDY
A large enamelware
bucket conveniently
contains supplies
(gardening gloves, for
example) and keeps the
garden hose kink-free.

Stop and Smell the...

Azalea

Rhododendron

WHY WE LOVE THEM
With their showy color (purple, pink, red, yellow), these low-maintenance shrubs epitomize spring in the South.

WHAT TO KNOW
The first American azaleas were planted in South Carolina at Middleton Place Gardens. Although azaleas are available as both evergreen or deciduous, the latter is the way to go if you're looking for the most vibrant color.

FAVORITE VARIETIES
The Piedmont, Alabama, and Florida Flame get high marks.

Magnolia

Magnolia grandiflora

WHY WE LOVE THEM
Where to start? Those fragrant ivory flowers, the shiny, waxy green leaves, their towering presence... (Smith County, Mississippi, boasts a stately 121-footer!)

WHAT TO KNOW
Small yards need not apply: A regular Southern magnolia typically grows up to 80 feet tall and 30 to 40 feet wide.

FAVORITE VARIETIES
In addition to the classic cited above, the ornamental Little Gem is a good option for tighter spaces.

Camellia

Camellia japonica

WHY WE LOVE THEM
While Alabama may claim this fragrant bloom, dubbed the "Peony of the South," as its state flower, the diplomatic camellia has no loyalties.

WHAT TO KNOW
These plants like partial shade (don't we all!) and grow well in rich, slightly acidic soil. Also noteworthy: The deer are disinterested.

FAVORITE VARIETIES
It's hard to pare down from more than 3,000 options, but Kramer's Surprise, White by the Gate, and Debutante are all frequently cited favorites.

Star Jasmine

Trachelospermum jasminoides

WHY WE LOVE IT
The flowering vine brings a perfume-like fragrance to a Southern garden.

WHAT TO KNOW
From a different family than true jasmines, this fast-growing, five-petaled evergreen perennial is a popular option for lattices, fences, and pergolas.

FAVORITE VARIETIES
The main difference here is flower color. White is the most common, but Pink Air and Star of Tuscany (yellow) deliver bolder blooms.

FOR THE LOVE OF...

Peggy Martin Roses

This hardy climbing rose is named after a Louisiana gardener whose home was submerged in 20 feet of water during Hurricane Katrina. Only two plants survived: a Crinum and a then-unnamed semi-thornless rose. Texas A&M professor Dr. Bill Welch went on to name the rose, which is now considered a symbol of resiliency.

Perfect the Porch Planter

A landscape designer by trade, Georgia native Carmen Johnston is especially skilled at eye-catching container gardens. Here are some of her tactics.

Think outside the pot. Carmen's favorite unexpected vessels for planting include plastic-lined French boulangerie baskets (shown on left), wide and shallow French copper jam pots, and antique chicken feeders with lots of compartments.

Follow the three *T*s. For a visual mix, incorporate elements that are thick, tall, and trailing (also known in Southern circles as the "thriller, filler, and spiller" strategy). Stuff plants in (here, geraniums, phlox, and petunias) for a lush look. Plant tall bloomers (here, delphinium) in the back for height, and add ivy along the edges for a trailing effect.

Keep it damp. The soil should be moist but not soggy. Setting the vessel in a saucer or lipped tray also allows you to add water from the bottom.

More Thriller, Filler, and Spiller

Three Southern gardeners share their go-to container combos.

"For shady spots, I love **Green Spice heuchera** [thriller], **impatiens** [filler], and **moneywort** [spiller]." —*Jennifer Gibson, The Good Earth Garden Center, Little Rock, Arkansas*

"I pair specialty cut pink and orange **daffodils** [thriller] with **apple mint** [filler] and **everbearing strawberries** [spiller]," —*Farmer-florist Dee Hall, Norfolk, Virginia*

"I love the surprise of edible options: **rosemary** [thriller], **buttercrunch lettuce** [filler], and a **white sweet alyssum** [spiller]." —*Emily Grohovsky, Cedar Hill Gardens, Madison, Mississippi*

DISPLAY YOUR DOGWOODS

A symbol of new life and hope, the flowering dogwood (*Cornus florida*)
is considered the South's most tried-and-true ornamental tree.
(No wonder Virginia and North Carolina both declared the dogwood the state
flower.) When the first branches blossom, gather a cluster in a vintage fishing
creel (lined with plastic and a wet floral foam base to keep pieces secure).

From the Kitchen

"Over the years since I left home, I have kept thinking about the people I grew up with and about our way of life. I realize how much the bond that held us had to do with food."
—**Chef and Virginia native Edna Lewis**

The Southern Checklist

Make Pimento Cheese Deviled Eggs

·····◇·····

Dish Out Brandied Strawberry Shortcakes

It's all about the mayo ratio.

·····◇·····

Try Chicken Salad, Five Ways

·····◇·····

Serve Up Shrimp and Grits

It's a Southern staple for good reason.

·····◇·····

Bake a Hummingbird Bundt Cake

TRAY CHIC

Designed to showcase these creamy creations by the dozen, deviled egg platters began appearing on tables in the mid-1900s. At local antiques shops, you can find vintage versions from makers like Johnson Brothers and Pfaltzgraff.

Keep 'em Appetized

Pimento Cheese Deviled Eggs

It was in the early 1900s—when shelf-stable mayo and electric refrigerators became mainstays—that the deviled egg got its crack at snack stardom.

WORKING TIME *25 minutes*   **TOTAL TIME** *40 minutes*   **MAKES** *12 servings*

12 **large eggs**

½ **cup mayonnaise**

1½ **tablespoons fresh lemon juice**

1 **teaspoon hot sauce**

Kosher salt

⅓ **cup diced pimentos**

1 **ounce extra-sharp Cheddar, finely grated (about ¼ cup)**

1 **scallion, finely chopped, plus more for garnish**

1. Place the eggs in a large saucepan, adding enough cold water to cover by 2 inches. Bring to a boil. Remove from heat, cover, and let stand for 11 minutes.

2. Drain the eggs and return them to the pan. Gently shake the pan until the eggshells are cracked all over. Run the eggs under cold water, then peel them and discard the shells.

3. Halve the eggs lengthwise, then scoop the yolks into a bowl and set the whites aside. To the bowl with the yolks, add the mayonnaise, lemon juice, hot sauce, and ½ teaspoon salt. Mash with a fork to combine. Add pimentos, Cheddar, and scallion. Stir to combine. Spoon or pipe the yolk mixture into the egg whites and garnish with more scallions.

A SHORT HISTORY OF...

Southern Brunch

Although it was British writer Guy Beringer whose case for "brunch" first appeared in an 1895 edition of *Hunter's Weekly,* you could say the meal was popularized (and, *ahem,* perfected) stateside in New Orleans. During the late 1800s, the legendary Madame Bégué, proprietor of H. Bégué's Exchange (later Tujague's) on Decatur Street—located across from the legendary French Market—became known for serving "second breakfast" at 11 a.m. to butchers, dockhands, and other market workers finishing their dawn shifts. It turns out that "second" breakfast concept also appealed to late-night carousers, and it soon took hold citywide. Modern-day visitors to New Orleans can continue the tradition at can't-miss brunch spots like Commander's Palace.

Raid the Garden

Brandied Strawberry Shortcakes

It's commonly understood that biscuits make everything better, even more so when they're paired with in-season strawberries and malted whipped cream.

WORKING TIME *30 minutes* **TOTAL TIME** *1 hour* **MAKES** *6 servings*

FOR THE BRANDIED STRAWBERRIES

- 2 (16-ounce) containers strawberries, trimmed and quartered
- ½ cup granulated sugar
- ¼ cup Cognac or other aged brandy

FOR THE BISCUITS

- 4 cups "00" Pizza Flour (or 2⅔ cups all-purpose flour and 1⅓ cups cake flour), plus more for work surface
- ¾ cup granulated sugar
- 1½ teaspoons kosher salt
- 4 teaspoons baking powder
- 1 teaspoon baking soda
- ¾ cup (1½ sticks) cold unsalted butter, cut into pieces
- 1½ cups buttermilk

Turbinado sugar, for sprinkling

FOR THE WHIPPED CREAM

- 2 cups heavy cream
- 2 tablespoons granulated sugar
- 2 tablespoons malted milk powder
- ½ teaspoon pure vanilla extract

1. Make the brandied strawberries: Mash one-fourth of the strawberries in a bowl with a fork. Stir in remaining berries, granulated sugar, and cognac. Cover and refrigerate at least 30 minutes and up to 3 hours.

2. Make the biscuits: Preheat the oven to 450°F. Sift together flour, granulated sugar, salt, baking powder, and baking soda in a bowl. Cut in butter using two forks or a pastry blender until it forms pea-size pieces. Stir in buttermilk and gently mix until a shaggy ball forms.

3. Turn dough out onto a lightly floured work surface. With floured hands, knead 2 to 3 times. Pat or roll into a 1-inch-thick circle. Cut dough into 4 wedges, and stack the pieces on top of each other. Roll again into a 1-inch-thick circle. Repeat 2 more times.

4. Cut biscuits with a 2½-inch round cutter; reroll scraps once. Place on a baking sheet, touching slightly. Sprinkle with turbinado sugar and freeze 15 minutes. Bake until golden brown, 18 to 20 minutes. Transfer to a wire rack to cool.

5. Make the whipped cream: Beat cream, granulated sugar, malted milk powder, and vanilla with an electric mixer on medium speed until soft peaks form, 1 to 2 minutes.

6. Halve biscuits and top with berries and whipped cream, dividing evenly. Replace the tops of biscuits, if desired, and serve immediately.

Ask a Southerner
TURNING FOOD INTO FELLOWSHIP

Chef **Erika Council**, owner of Atlanta's Bomb Biscuit Co., on the power of a shared dish

"My granny Geraldine carried her then-rare advanced degree from Columbia University back home with her to the small town of Goldsboro, North Carolina. It was there that she became a 'church mother' personified. Feeding people was her ministry, and she manned the church kitchen as though it were a Michelin-starred restaurant. The flow resembled an assembly line, with plates and silverware at the beginning and biscuits and drinks at the end. My grandmother made sure I knew the origins of the sanctity of church dinners, which helped fund the fight for equal rights. She once told me a story from her time up north, when she shared a basket of biscuits with a white couple who sat next to her. They got to chatting. Being from the Jim Crow South, she was amazed that they could simply eat and talk together. I now own a bakery in the Old Fourth Ward area of Atlanta, best known as the birthplace of MLK, Jr., and I think of that story of togetherness when I make biscuits. I take pride in setting a table for everyone, just like Granny taught me."

Try a Twist on a Classic

Chicken Salad, Five Ways

———— ◇ ————

Dill or no dill? Curried or classic? No self-respecting Southerner can go
without a signature spin on this ladies luncheon mainstay.

WORKING TIME *20 to 35 minutes*   **TOTAL TIME** *35 minutes (including chicken)*   **MAKES** *4 servings*

Poached Chicken

Fill a medium saucepan halfway with water; bring to a boil. Add 1 teaspoon **kosher salt** and 1½ pounds small boneless, skinless **chicken breasts.** Reduce heat and simmer, until cooked through, 12 to 15 minutes. Transfer to a plate; cool completely. Shred or chop into pieces. *Makes 3 cups.*

No. 1
Updated Classic Chicken Salad

Whisk together ½ cup **mayonnaise** and 2 tablespoons **pickle brine** in a bowl. Season with salt and pepper. Add ½ cup **chopped pickles,** 2 stalks sliced **celery,** 2 tablespoons chopped fresh **flat-leaf parsley,** 2 tablespoons chopped fresh **dill,** and **Poached Chicken;** toss to combine.

No. 2
Curry Chicken Salad

Whisk together ¼ cup low-fat **sour cream,** 2 tablespoons **mayonnaise,** 1 teaspoon **lemon zest,** 2 tablespoons **lemon juice,** and 1 tablespoon **curry powder** in a bowl. Season with **salt** and **pepper.** Add two **scallions** (thinly sliced), ¼ cup fresh chopped **cilantro,** ½ cup **golden raisins,** and **Poached Chicken;** toss to combine.

No. 3
Thai-Style Chicken Salad

Whisk together 6 tablespoons fresh **lime juice,** 2 tablespoons **fish sauce,** 1 tablespoon **canola oil,** and 2 teaspoons **honey** in a bowl. Season with **salt** and **pepper.** Add ¼ cup chopped **red onion,** ½ large chopped **Granny Smith apple,** 4 small **radishes** (cut into matchsticks), 2 tablespoons fresh **mint,** ⅓ cup chopped **roasted peanuts,** and **Poached Chicken;** toss to combine.

No. 4
Mediterranean Chicken Salad

Whisk together 3 tablespoons **olive oil,** 2½ tablespoons **red wine vinegar,** and 1 tablespoon **Dijon mustard** in a bowl. Season with **kosher salt** and freshly **ground black pepper.** Add 2 thinly sliced **scallions,** 3 tablespoons chopped fresh **flat-leaf parsley,** ¼ cup pitted **green olives** (roughly chopped), ¼ cup chopped **roasted almonds,** and **Poached Chicken;** toss to combine.

No. 5
Pesto Chicken Salad

Whisk together ½ cup store-bought **pesto,** ¼ cup low-fat **Greek yogurt,** 2 teaspoons **lemon zest,** and 1 tablespoon **lemon juice** in a bowl. Add ¼ cup **toasted pine nuts** and **Poached Chicken;** toss to combine.

Serve a Southern Supper

Shrimp and Grits

———◇———

While traditionally served for breakfast or brunch, this staple of
Low Country cuisine is a solid around-the-clock contender.

WORKING TIME *30 minutes*   **TOTAL TIME** *1 hour*   **MAKES** *4 to 6 servings*

2 **green poblano peppers, halved and seeded**

1 **cup white stone-ground grits**

2 **ounces extra-sharp Cheddar, coarsely grated (about ½ cup)**

2 **tablespoons unsalted butter**

Kosher salt and freshly ground black pepper

2 **tablespoons olive oil, divided**

1 **small onion, sliced**

1 **small red pepper, sliced**

2 **cloves garlic, sliced**

1 **pound shrimp, peeled and deveined**

½ **teaspoon ground coriander**

Pinch cayenne pepper

2 **cups chicken broth**

½ **to 1 cup whole milk**

Fresh cilantro leaves and lime wedges, for serving

1. Preheat broiler. Place poblano peppers, cut sides down, on a rimmed baking sheet. Broil until charred, 2 to 4 minutes. Transfer to a bowl, cover, and let cool. Discard skins; dice peppers.

2. Bring 4 cups water to a boil in a large pot. Slowly whisk in grits. Reduce heat and simmer, stirring often (grits will bubble in spots), until liquid is absorbed and grits are tender, 20 to 25 minutes. Remove from heat and stir in Cheddar and butter. Season with salt.

3. Heat 1 tablespoon oil in a large skillet over medium heat. Add onion and red pepper. Cook, stirring occasionally, until just tender, 6 to 8 minutes. Add garlic and cook, stirring occasionally, 1 minute. Transfer to a bowl; reserve skillet.

4. Season shrimp with coriander, cayenne pepper, salt, and black pepper. Heat remaining tablespoon oil in reserved skillet over medium heat. Add shrimp and cook until opaque throughout, 2 to 3 minutes per side; transfer to bowl with vegetables. Add broth to skillet, increase heat to medium-high, and cook until liquid is reduced to 1 cup, 8 to 9 minutes. Return shrimp, vegetables, and poblanos to skillet and toss to combine.

5. Return grits to medium heat. Add ½ cup milk. Cook, stirring often, until heated through, 3 to 4 minutes (add additional milk up to ½ cup to thin, if necessary). Serve grits topped with shrimp mixture with cilantro and lime wedges alongside.

Hummingbird Cake

This so-called Southern confection can be traced south—*way south*—to Jamaica, where the doctorbird (a hummingbird species) is the national bird. In the 1960s, in an attempt to showcase Caribbean flavors such as banana and pineapple, the Jamaica Tourist Board mailed press kits with a "Doctorbird Cake" recipe to the U.S. Subsequently, the recipe popped up at church socials and in community cookbooks, but it wasn't until 1978, when North Carolina resident Mrs. L.H. Wiggins had her recipe published in a national magazine, that Hummingbird Cake took hold across the South. That same year, a hummingbird cake won the blue ribbon at the Kentucky State Fair.

Bring Out the Cake Stand

Hummingbird Bundt Cake

———— ◦ ————

Featuring edible pineapple "flowers," this classic Bundt cake is
sure to be a sideboard staple for decades to come.

WORKING TIME *45 minutes*   **TOTAL TIME** *4 hours 30 minutes*   **MAKES** *1 cake (12 servings)*

FOR THE PINEAPPLE FLOWERS

- 1 **whole pineapple**

FOR THE CAKE

- 3 **cups all-purpose flour, spooned and leveled, plus more for the pan**
- 1 **cup granulated sugar**
- 1 **cup packed light brown sugar**
- 1 **teaspoon ground cinnamon**
- 1 **teaspoon baking soda**

Kosher salt

- 3 **large eggs**
- 2 **cups coarsely mashed ripe bananas (about 4 to 6 bananas)**
- 1 **(8-ounce) can crushed pineapple in juice, undrained**
- ½ **cup (1 stick) unsalted butter, melted, plus more for the pan**
- ½ **cup vegetable oil**
- 2 **teaspoons pure vanilla extract**
- 1 **cup chopped pecans, toasted**

FOR THE GLAZE

- 4 **ounces cream cheese, at room temperature**
- ¼ **cup (½ stick) unsalted butter, at room temperature**
- 2 **cups confectioners' sugar**
- 1 **teaspoon pure vanilla extract**
- 2 **to 4 tablespoons milk**

Small fresh flowers, for decorative garnish

1. Make the pineapple flowers: Preheat the oven to 250°F. Line a rimmed baking sheet with parchment paper. Cut ½ inch off the top and bottom of the pineapple, then peel it. Scoop out the eyes with a ¼ measuring teaspoon. Using a mandoline, slice 12 (1/16-inch-thick) slices of pineapple and pat dry. (Reserve the remaining pineapple for another use.)

2. Arrange the slices in a single layer on the prepared baking sheet. Bake, flipping slices halfway through, 1 hour. Slices should be dry and lightly browned on the edges. If not, continue baking, flipping every 15 minutes. Carefully press 1 slice into each cup of a muffin tin, with the edges cupped upward. Cool at room temperature at least 8 hours and up to overnight.

3. Make the cake: Preheat the oven to 325°F. Butter and flour a 10-inch (12-cup) Bundt pan. In a large bowl, whisk together the flour, granulated sugar, brown sugar, cinnamon, baking soda, and 1 teaspoon salt. In a separate bowl, whisk together the eggs, bananas, crushed pineapple and juice, melted butter, oil, and vanilla. Add the banana-pineapple mixture to the flour mixture, stirring just until combined. Stir in pecans. Transfer the batter to the prepared Bundt pan.

4. Bake until a toothpick inserted in the center comes out clean, 1 hour and 5 minutes to 1 hour and 10 minutes. Cool the cake in the pan on a wire rack for 15 minutes, then transfer the cake to a wire rack to cool completely.

5. Make the glaze: Beat the cream cheese and butter with an electric mixer on medium speed until creamy, 1 to 2 minutes. Reduce the speed to low and gradually beat in the confectioners' sugar. Beat in the vanilla and 2 tablespoons of the milk, adding more as needed to reach a thick but pourable consistency. Drizzle the glaze over the cake. Top with pineapple flowers and garnish with fresh flowers.

· SPRING ·

On the Go

---◆---

"In the spring, I have counted 136 kinds of weather inside of 24 hours."
—Author and Missouri native Mark Twain

The Southern Checklist

Explore Round Top, Texas

·····◆·····

Cowboy boots encouraged.

Visit a U-Pick Farm

Because you can never have too many dishes!

·····◆·····

Go Antiquing for Vintage China

◆ **PLUS** ◆

More Southern Wit & Wisdom

Mosquitoes, you've met your match.

HEEL COUNTRY
Adopted as the Texas State Footwear in 2007, the no-nonsense cowboy boot is a Southern wardrobe essential. (The chunky heels were designed to hang on to stirrups.)

INDULGE YOUR YONDERLUST

Round Top, Texas

The secret, it seems, is out. This tiny town—just one square mile with, last we checked, a total population of 87—now draws 100,000-plus shoppers every spring and fall for Texas Antiques Week (which, not to confuse matters, actually spans more than a week) and has year-round appeal. Conveniently nestled in the picturesque Hill Country between Austin and Houston, the map-dot destination has inspired endless comparisons—"the Hamptons of Houston," "the Cotswolds of Texas"—but visitors know Round Top is uniquely, well, Round Top. Where else can you find social media influencers holding up traffic to get a photo of a cow? Dressed-to-the-nines designers rushing into an antiques tent at the sound of a dinner bell? After perusing the old-world wares at well-curated venues like Marburger Farm, Blue Hills, Les Halles, and the Compound, be sure to check out the Round Top Festival Institute and Henkel Square Market before enjoying a slice of Texas Trash Pie at Royer's Pie Haven (above).

TALK LIKE A TEXAN

All Hat and No Cattle
Refers to someone full of big talk but no substance or action

Buc-ee's
A gas station beloved for its clean bathrooms and puffed beaver nuggets

Gig 'Em
The gesture and expression associated with the Texas A&M Aggies

Hook 'Em
The chant and signal of the University of Texas at Austin

Kolache
A popular Lone Star state pastry brought over by Czech immigrants

REASONS TO LOVE
Round Top

No. 1
Bluebonnets

What the shamrock is to Ireland, this wildflower is to Texas, and late March into April is prime time to frolic in the fields among its blooms. (Just watch out for those longhorns, okay?)

No. 2
Stylish Spaces

There's no shortage of cool spots to bunk up around town, including the Frenchie, the Wander Inn, and Hotel Lulu (pictured).

No. 3
Charming Boot-iques

Local spots like Townsend Provisions stay stocked with all sorts of country wares, including preloved cowboy boots.

No. 4
Starry Nights

Gather around the fire or a farm table at the 20-acre retreat Rancho Pillow, or check out the twice-annual Junk Prom, a chiffon-a-thon hosted by sisters Amie Sikes and Jolie Sikes-Smith, featuring food, live music, and dancing. Corsages optional.

More Small Towns to Explore in Spring

COVINGTON, LOUISIANA
In the seat of St. Tammany Parish, Big Easy livin' beckons with art festivals, historic general stores, and wetlands full of wildlife wonders.

THOMASVILLE, GEORGIA
Known as the "City of Roses," this southwest town just 35 miles north of Tallahassee is best visited during the 100-years-strong rose festival in late April.

BEAUFORT, SOUTH CAROLINA
In the Spanish moss–drenched Low Country, Beaufort's entire downtown is designated a historic district by the National Trust for Historic Preservation.

Visit a U-Pick Farm

———◆———

This seasonal sojourn, which is best enjoyed in spring and summer (see: muscadines)—was born out of necessity. After World War I, a perfect storm of declining birth rates, ballooning debts, and dwindling needs for U.S. agricultural products abroad left farmers desperate to sell surplus produce. At the same time, city dwellers were eager to hit the freshly paved roads that newly connected urban centers to the countryside. The solution? Rebrand the labor of fruit picking into a leisure activity! Vacationers were heavily encouraged to detour to nearby farms for an afternoon of fruit-focused fun. Almost a century later, a trip to a U-pick farm is a Southern rite—and bite—of passage.

FOR THE LOVE OF...

Fruity Water Towers

Talk about a pit stop. If you've ever traveled between Charlotte and Atlanta, no doubt you've laid eyes on the Gaffney, South Carolina, icon known as "the Peachoid," aka "the Peach," a 135-foot-tall, 1 million-gallon tower that has been turning heads since its 1981 construction. Further west, along Alabama's I-65, you'll see its distant, slightly smaller cousin (built by the same company), the 120-foot-tall Big Peach, a 500,000-gallon tower off exit 212. (Don't miss the nearby Durbin Farms Market.) Still, it's not all peaches in these parts. In **Plant City, Florida,** you'll find a bulbous 500,000-gallon strawberry sweetening the landscape. Built in the 1920s, it's an ode to the city's berry farming heritage.

PICK YOUR PRODUCE

....

Strawberries

PEAK SEASON
As early as February in Florida, although generally late April through June

WHERE TO PICK
Oak Haven Farms & Winery in Sorrento, Florida, lets you enjoy the fruits of your labor at a picnic table situated beneath a picturesque oak tree. With face-painting and activities, Mrs. Heather's Farm in Albany, Louisiana, caters to kids and families.

HARVESTING TIP
Select full, firm berries. Grasp the stem just above the berry between the forefinger and the thumbnail, twist, and pull.

Blackberries

PEAK SEASON
May to July

WHERE TO PICK
The first commercial blackberry growers in Georgia, Southern Grace Farms in Enigma also allows guests to give it a go in their designated U-pick field. Family-run since 1839, Circle S Farms in Lebanon, Tennessee, offers all sorts of picking options and has an on-site smokehouse.

HARVESTING TIP
Wear pants and long sleeves because things can get thorny out there! A ripe blackberry will be plump and black, not purple or red.

Peaches

PEAK SEASON
May to September

WHERE TO PICK
McCraw Farms happily welcomes visitors in Alabama's Chilton County (home of the peach water tower). Just 30 miles south of Atlanta's Southern Belle Farm offers 10 peach varieties and an annual U-pick pass.

HARVESTING TIP
Look for peaches that give slightly when pressed; overly firm fruit isn't quite ripe. Lift the peach upward and pull gently to separate it from the tree; peaches that require a forceful pull to pick aren't fully ripe.

Muscadines

PEAK SEASON
You'll have to wait until July for these thick-skinned grapes, which last into October. (Note: The fun-to-say scuppernong grape is a variety of muscadine.)

WHERE TO PICK
Muscadines are the official fruit of North Carolina, so head to the Tarheel State—Benjamin Vineyards in Graham, Cauble Creek Vineyards in Salisbury, or Griffin Vineyards in Sanford—for prime produce and, yes, that famed muscadine wine.

HARVESTING TIP
Look for darker grapes that are easy to pull from the vine.

A SHORT HISTORY OF...

The Honor Stand

Southern farmers have long relied on the tradition of setting out produce alongside a list of prices, a ledger, and an unsupervised box for payment. While not a perfect system, farmers who use it have psychology on their side: Researchers have found that acts of trust-building—even with strangers you don't interact with—induce the release of oxytocin, which can cause surges in generosity. Guess that's why honor stand shoppers tend to overpay!

HOME PLATES
Replacements Ltd., the nation's largest china warehouse, is based in McLeansville, North Carolina, and features a whopping 425,000 patterns!

Go Antiquing for Vintage China

It is a truth universally acknowledged that a Southerner in possession of fine china must show it off. It is also true that it is impossible to be in possession of too many patterns. Southerners, after all, love a good theme, and this particular season—with all of its garden-club gatherings and celebratory showers and Mother's Day merriment—serves up ample excuses to reach for, say, a rose motif or tobacco leaf.

Perhaps that's precisely why spring party season coincides with antiquing season. Now is peak time to supplement your tabletop assortment by visiting an antiques show, estate sale, or other approved purveyor of patina.

From feminine chintz to fanciful English roses, here are some of the most popular spring-friendly patterns to ever grace a Southern table. (Oh, the things they've overheard!)

NO. 1

Tobacco Leaf

The 18th-century's most coveted pattern was first developed in China circa 1780. (The original manufacturer remains unknown.) Today, the design is made by **Mottahedeh** using 27 colors and 22-karat gold.

NO. 2

Azalea

Created by Japanese maker **Noritake** in 1918, this pattern was offered by the Larkin Soap Company to customers who ordered products by mail. Discontinued in 1941, when U.S. imports halted during World War II, Azalea got a short-lived second act from 1988 to 1992.

NO. 3

Desert Rose

The most-sold dinnerware in U.S. history, this pattern was introduced by **Franciscan** in 1941. Pieces from those early days (California backstamp 1941–1984) are worth more than those made after the company was purchased by Wedgwood, which moved production to Europe in 1985.

NO. 4

Old Country Roses

English maker **Royal Albert** launched this pattern in 1962. A heavy hitter since its introduction, the pattern has gone on to sell more than 130 million pieces, making it the company's most successful design.

SPRING WIT & WISDOM

More ways to embrace the season around these pollen-filled parts.

Write a Better Thank-You Note

GET PERSONAL.
"Select note cards that speak to your interests," says Jennifer Hunt, founder of Southern stationery brand Dogwood Hill, which offers 1,000 customizable options.

MIND THE STOCK.
"Our standard is 120-pound paper, which is nice and thick," she says.

SKIP THE SCRIPT.
"You don't want it to feel copied and pasted," says Jennifer. Cite the item received and how you plan to use it. ("I'm over the moon about my new cast-iron skillet. I can't wait to try my hand at Aunt Lottie's famous biscuits.")

GET A GOOD PEN.
"It makes note-writing more special, and it somehow makes my penmanship look better," she says.

DESIGN WITH A DRAWL

Warm Up Your Welcome

Give your front door a more colorful personality with these picks from Southern designers.

Restful by *Sherwin-Williams*
"It's the perfect spring green—happy but neutral enough to mix well with accent colors."
—*Brian Patrick Flynn, Atlanta*

True Blue by *Benjamin Moore*
"It's like the perfect summer day with beautiful blue skies. For extra depth, go for a high-gloss finish."
—*Loi Thai, Annapolis, Maryland*

Warming Peach by *Benjamin Moore*
"It's cheery but still understated and pretty, especially when paired with soft coral blooms like ranunculus." —*Erika Powell, Islamorada, Florida*

SOUNDTRACK

Compile a Playlist

Singer-songwriter Robert Earl King ("The Front Porch Song") shares his porchin' preferences.

"Big City"
by Merle Haggard

"Gentle on My Mind"
by John Hartford

"Soak Up the Sun"
by Sheryl Crow

"Summer Breeze"
by Seals and Crofts

"Someday Soon"
by Judy Collins

"Carey"
by Joni Mitchell

"The Poet Game"
by Greg Brown

"Streets of Bakersfield"
by Dwight Yoakam and Buck Owens

"Dust My Broom"
by Freddie King

IDENTIFICATION KEY

Picket Fences

To keep critters in (or out!) but still allow for easy banter with passersby, keep the height to 48 inches max.

Dog Ear

Inverted Dog Ear

French Gothic

Gothic

SPRING HAPPENINGS

There's no shortage of ways to revel in the region.

Houston Livestock Show and Rodeo
Houston

Enjoy concerts, carnival rides, and 'cue at the world's largest livestock exhibition.

St. Patrick's Day Parade
Savannah

This 200-years-strong ode to Ireland's patron saint is one of the largest in America.

New Orleans Jazz and Heritage Festival
New Orleans

Also known as "Jazz Fest," this two-week event draws more than a half-million people and 600 bands.

National Cornbread Festival
South Pittsburg, Tennessee

This tribute to a skillet staple takes place in the same town where Lodge cast iron is handcrafted.

Interstate Mullet Toss
Perdido Key, Florida

The Flora-Bama beach bar hosts this contest that involves throwing a dead mullet over the Alabama-Florida state line. Yep, you read that right.

SOUTHERNISMS, EXPLAINED

"Madder than a Wet Hen"

When hens sit on eggs, they can have periods of broodiness, when they get aggressively protective. Farmers would often dunk them in cold water to temper the 'tude.

ONLY IN THE SOUTH...

10-SECOND SERMONS

Even if you don't make it to the local Sunday service, you'll find little lessons in these ubiquitous block letters spotted outside churches down country roads with witty one-liners like "Tweet others as you want to be tweeted," "Prayer: The best wireless connection," and "God does not have favorites, but the sign guy does. Roll Tide!"

HOME REMEDY

Ward off Those Pesky Mosquitoes

Like the Capulets and Montagues, Southerners and mosquitoes have never gotten along. To keep them at bay in a decorative way, place 4 lemon slices, 3 rosemary sprigs, and 10 drops of eucalyptus or mint essential oil in a mason jar. Add water nearly to the rim and stir; top with a floating candle.

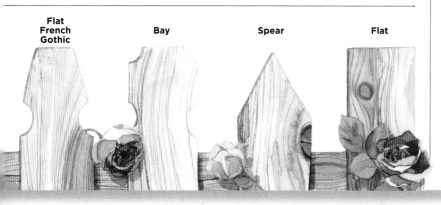

Flat French Gothic   Bay   Spear   Flat

ROAD DRIP

Spanish moss is not, in fact, Spanish (it's native to the United States), nor is it moss (it's a flowering plant), but it sure is magical.

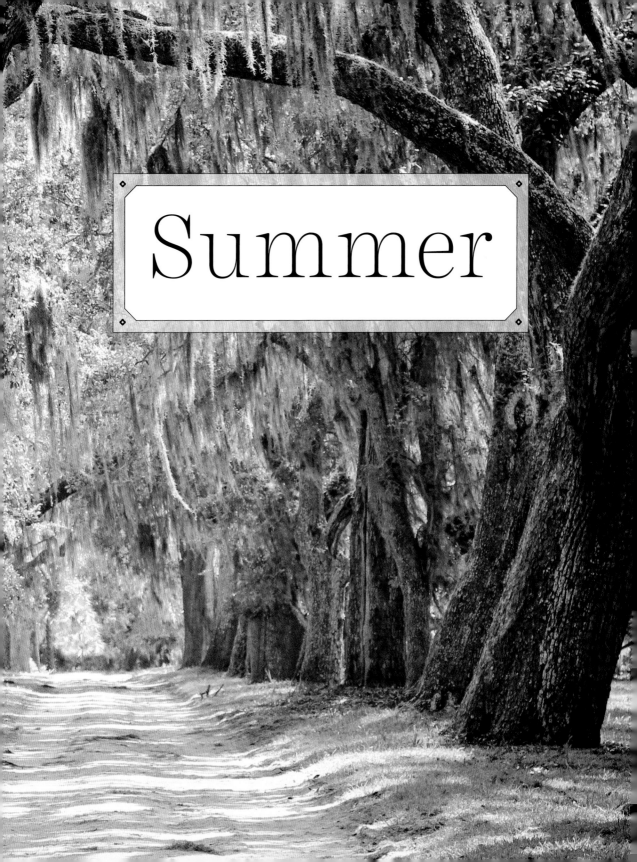

Summer

It's Not *Summer* in the South Without...

·····◇·····

Escaping to your
favorite hidden-secret
Southern swimming hole
(You know just the one.)

◇

That first backyard dinner
when the fireflies pay a
visit—and the catch-and-
release magic that ensues

◇

The humble beauty of
a tire swing hanging from a
sturdy branch—and
all the free-range frolicking
it represents

◇

Chins dripping with the juice
of farmstand watermelon

◇

Bringing home $1 sunflower
stems from the U-pick farm

◇

Biting into an heirloom tomato
sandwich right over the sink

◇

Braking for soaked-through
bags of boiled peanuts

◇

Puttin' up the seasonal
bumper crop
to enjoy year-round

· SUMMER ·

Around the House

*"It's important to me that my home feel welcoming.
I want people to feel like they can sit on the furniture.
You can have a beautiful house, very well decorated,
but you have to be able to sit down, or else it's not a home."*
—**Actress and Tennesseean Reese Witherspoon**

Having a
pony in the
yard helps!

The Southern Checklist

Create a Brake-Worthy Porch

Rethink Screen Time

Design a Breezy Bedroom

Go Wild with Gingham

It's not just for
tablecloths.

Create a Brake-Worthy Porch

There are certain things that tend to stop Southerners in their tracks, with fresh peaches and charm-packed Southern exteriors topping the list. Whether it's a cute Colonial, a colorful Creole cottage, or a stately Georgian, we're prone to pumping the brakes and dropping our jaws. (Perhaps now is as good a time as any to apologize to the cars caught behind us.)

To be fair, we can't help it: There are certain sights that make our hearts skip a beat, and bedding designer Bailey McCarthy's Victorian farmhouse in Bellville, Texas, is about as picturesque as it gets, with scalloped shingles, a Dutch door, and a sprawling front porch. Frame the scene with a perfectly placed live oak and a miniature pony, and we may feel compelled to knock on the door. (Don't say we didn't warn you.)

NO. 1
Stately Tree

Historically, live oaks have only grown as far north as lower Virginia, which is why they've become a distinctly Southern symbol of strength.

NO. 2
White Paint

There's a reason so many farmhouses are white. It began with whitewash, aka "lime paint," which was used during Colonial times to prevent mildew.

NO. 3
Metal Roof

Withstanding their fair share of Southern storms, these durable roofs have long been a staple in this region. For a classic look, go with a standing seam style.

NO. 4
Pink Door

A vibrant entrance is the architectural equivalent of a neighborly wave. (Shown: Cat's Meow by Benjamin Moore.)

REFRESHER COURSE

TEXAS RANCH WATER

Traditionally a mix of tequila, lime juice, and soda water, this West Texas tipple has taken over the South. To make your own, spread kosher salt on a flat plate. Rub the rim of a 12-ounce glass with a cut **lime,** then dip the rim in **salt.** Fill the glass with **ice** and top with ½ ounce **fresh lime juice** and 1½ ounces **blanco tequila;** stir to combine. Top with **Topo Chico.** (Fun fact: Bottled since 1895, the bubbly mineral water is sourced from an inactive volcano in Mexico.)

Rethink Screen Time

GRAND SLAM
The average screen door slam is 80 decibels, which is basically a whisper compared to the 100-decibel chirp of some crickets.

Know-How

GUSSY UP A SCREEN DOOR

Add a little flourish to a run-of-the-mill builder-grade door with these ideas.

EASIEST
No saw or drill needed for this project, which simply calls for screws and corner brackets and headers.

EASY
Using a hacksaw, cut ¾-inch square dowels to create panes, and attach four fan brackets to make a circle. Add a gallery rail and spandrel for horizontal strips.

EASY-ISH
Using a chop saw, cut two 36- by ¾-inch square dowels (available at home-improvement stores) at 45-degree angles, and place as shown.

Nothing complements the come-and-go casualness of summer like the mesh mainstay known as a screen door. A door, by definition, is a barrier. But a screen door is an invitation. It's a way to remain reachable—to keep the outside world within hollering distance, even when you're safely ensconced away from midsummer sun as the kids cartwheel through the sprinkler. Screened doors were born out of practicality—early versions were made of cheesecloth to keep insects at bay—but we suspect they'd still find their place in a world without pests. A screen door makes it possible to savor the chirping of crickets, or to relish the pitter-patter of a rainy afternoon, but no sound may be more welcome than the late-night *creeeeak* that signifies a loved one has returned home.

DESIGN A BREEZY BEDROOM

No. 1
SWEET HOME ALABAMA
Featuring scalloped shams and florals, this Birmingham space is a botanical garden in bed form.

No. 2
TEXAS TWANG
The iconic violet hues of the state flower lend themselves to a purple-blue bedroom. (An on-theme hooked pillow helps, too.)

No. 3
LOW COUNTRY LEISURE
A sea of coastal blues with winks of wild grass–inspired greens nods to South Carolina's lush landscape.

No. 4
BLUEGRASS BLISS
Kentucky bluegrass gets its name from its flower heads. Here, a scheme of blues plays well with a pine chest and a horse cutout.

Go Wild with Gingham

Gingham's Checkered Past

1943
The folksy charm (and wardrobe) of *Oklahoma!* takes Broadway.

1950s
Rockabilly music becomes popular, giving gingham some edge.

1964
Farm girl Mary Ann Summers checks in to *Gilligan's Island.*

As far as patterns go, checks have a straightforward graphic charm that's pleasing to the eye and a well-proven longevity (checked gingham dates back to the 17th century, after all). You can hardly go a day in the region without encountering some form of the pattern, whether it's a humble sink skirt (above) or a tablecloth at a meat-and-three. "Gingham has long been the workhorse of Southern design," says Callie Jenschke, cofounder of Supply, a Texas-based fabric and wallcovering showroom. "It's traditional but at the same time fresh, which is why we like to push designers and homeowners to use gingham as a basic. Gingham really works in any design." Depending on color, scale, and fabric heft, the timeless textile can indeed feel equally at home in a farmhouse or mountain cabin as it can in a stately Georgian or traditional Tudor. You could say it checks all the boxes.

No. 1
ON THE WALLS
A beige gingham
wallcovering charms
up a North Carolina
kitchen with green
cabinets.

No. 2
IN THE BEDROOM
A tailored gingham
bed proves
that checks can
skew more polished
than pastoral.

No. 3
ON A SOFA
In a Texas farmhouse,
a sofa outfitted in
cheerful red gingham
serves up classic
country comfort.

No. 4
AS A SKIRT
Simple curtains and
a coordinating skirt
in a sunny yellow
complement warm
wood cabin walls.

At the Table

"You know it's a great dinner party when time flows by so fast that all the sudden your 12-inch taper candles are only one inch."
—Author and Dallas resident Kimberly Whitman

The Southern Checklist

Set a Southern Farm Table

They're all cookout approved!

Pick Your Place Setting

Arrange a Seasonal Centerpiece

Host the Ultimate Summer Fish Fry

Hush puppies are a nonnegotiable.

Set a Southern Farm Table

———◇———

The South serves up no shortage of dreamy alfresco surroundings, whether it's moss-drenched oak trees in Savannah's Forsyth Park, the white-sand beaches of Florida's Highway 30A, or the majestic magnolias of Natchez, Mississippi. That's why it should come as no surprise that Southerners fancy any excuse to twirl up a table outdoors. And, despite the unpredictable weather and the inevitable mosquitoes, we're not afraid to take things up a notch. Take, for example, this Virginia spread set amid a field of sunflowers, dreamed up by designer Heather Chadduck Hillegas. The blue-and-white scheme complements the sunny golds and puts the "special" in special occasion.

NO. 1
Silver Candlesticks

Bring out the good stuff! Antique candlesticks add sheen to the table and a pretty flicker at sundown.

NO. 2
Layered Linens

An outdoor setting is no reason to skimp on textiles. Here, a ground-grazing tablecloth plays well with four other fabrics.

NO. 3
Basket of Blankets

Should temperatures drop in the evening, a stash of lightweight throws allows guests to remain comfortable.

NO. 4
Clipper Place Cards

To tie in the scenery and encourage guests to bring home a few blooms, Heather placed garden shears at each setting.

PICK YOUR PLACE SETTING

No. 1
WESTERN WHIMSY
Bandannas do double-duty as paisley-patterned napkins; place atop a galvanized charger and spatterware plate.

No. 2
FRESH SQUEEZE
Hosting a crab boil? Write a name on a lemon, pair with a claw cracker, and tuck flowers into an Old Bay seasoning tin.

No. 3
CORN FED
Vintage cob holders also make for cute utensil trays. Place atop a red gingham napkin lined with white rickrack.

No. 4
PEACHY KEEN
Use a white paint pen to jot a name on a leaf plucked from the yard, and pair with a light orange plate. Place utensils in a mason jar.

Arrange a
Seasonal Centerpiece

◦

A favorite plant for container gardens and hanging baskets, geraniums
can also step up as a striking summer arrangement. When placed in
vintage potato chip tins and embellished with flags, these heat-tolerant
blooms deliver patriotic punch. (Extra points for procuring tins from
Southern-based brands such as Zapp's or Golden Flake.)

Host the Ultimate Summer Fish Fry

Pack up your tackle box and escape to your preferred
Southern swimmin' hole (here, Alabama's Smith Lake) to host a this
laid-back together that's perfect for the dock days of summer.

TIE ONE ON

For easy napkin "rings," bundle linens with twine and accent with vintage fishing bobbers.

A SHORT HISTORY OF...

The Hush Puppy

While there are conflicting stories on the origin of this cornmeal concoction, one of the more common anecdotes involves fishermen, who were said to use the deep-fried balls to quiet yappy dogs as they gathered 'round the campfire to cook up their fresh catch. Others say it was Confederate soldiers, who used the treats to quiet dogs as Yankees approached. Wherever their start, they're sure to quiet growling stomachs.

Crab Hush Puppies

MAKES *8 servings*
WORKING TIME *40 minutes*
TOTAL TIME *40 minutes*

Canola oil, for frying

- 1 **cup coarsely ground cornmeal**
- ½ **cup all-purpose flour, spooned and leveled**
- ¾ **teaspoon baking powder**
- ¾ **teaspoon kosher salt, plus more for garnish**
- ½ **teaspoon cayenne pepper**
- ¼ **teaspoon baking soda**
- 2 **scallions, finely chopped**
- 1 **tablespoon finely chopped fresh chives**
- 8 **ounces claw crabmeat (1½ cups), picked over**
- 4 **ounces Gruyère, grated (about 1 cup)**
- 1 **cup buttermilk**
- 1 **large egg**

1. Heat 1½ inches oil in a large Dutch oven over medium-high heat to 350°F (measure temperature with a deep-fry thermometer).

2. Meanwhile, whisk together cornmeal, flour, baking powder, salt, cayenne, and baking soda in a bowl. Add scallions and chives and whisk to combine. Add crabmeat and cheese and stir with a fork to combine. Make a well in the center, add buttermilk and egg, and mix until just combined.

3. Drop tablespoonfuls of batter into hot oil, being careful not to overcrowd the pot, and fry, turning occasionally, until golden brown, 3 to 5 minutes. Transfer to a paper towel–lined plate. Season with salt. Repeat with remaining batter.

Spicy Peach & Avocado Salad

MAKES *8 servings*
WORKING TIME *15 minutes*
TOTAL TIME *30 minutes*

- 3 **tablespoons fresh lemon juice**
- 3 **tablespoons olive oil**
- 2 **teaspoons pure honey**
- 1 **shallot, finely chopped**
- 1 **Fresno chile, thinly sliced**

Kosher salt and freshly ground black pepper

- 3 **ripe but firm peaches, cut into wedges**
- 2 **avocados, cut into wedges**
- ½ **cup fresh mint, torn if large, plus more for garnish**
- ¼ **cup roasted pistachios, chopped**

1. Whisk together lemon juice, oil, honey, shallot, and chile in a bowl. Season with salt and pepper. Add peaches and toss to coat. Let sit at least 15 minutes and up to 1 hour.

2. Just before serving, add avocado and mint and toss to combine. Season with salt and pepper. Top with pistachios and garnish with more mint.

Beer-Battered Seafood with Dipping Sauces

While seafood always tastes better when you've caught it (feet dangling off the dock with a rod in hand is part of the fun), if that's not an option, head to the local fish market and buy what's fresh!

MAKES *8 servings*   **WORKING TIME** *1 hour 30 minutes*   **TOTAL TIME** *1 hour 30 minutes*

Canola oil, for frying
- ½ **cup coarsely ground cornmeal**
- ½ **teaspoon paprika**
- ¼ **teaspoon baking soda**
- 1½ **cups all-purpose flour, divided**

Kosher salt and freshly ground black pepper
- 1 **(12-ounce) can lager-style beer**
- 1 **pound skinless cod or perch, cut into 8 strips**
- 1 **pound large (²¹⁄₂₅-count) peeled and deveined shrimp (tails left on)**
- 16 **clams, shucked**
- 1 **lemon, thinly sliced, plus wedges, for serving**

Chimichurri, Mignonette, prepared tartar sauce, hot sauce, and malt vinegar, for serving

1. Heat 1½ inches oil in a large Dutch oven over medium-high heat to 375°F (measure temperature with a deep-fry thermometer).

2. Meanwhile, whisk together cornmeal, paprika, baking soda, 1 cup flour, ½ teaspoon salt, and ½ teaspoon pepper in a bowl. Add beer and whisk to combine.

3. Place remaining ½ cup flour in a second bowl. Season with salt and pepper. Add fish, shrimp, clams, and lemon slices and toss to coat lightly.

4. Working with a few pieces at a time, remove seafood and lemons from flour, shaking off excess, and dip in batter, letting excess drip back into bowl. Carefully add to hot oil, being cautious not to overcrowd the pot. Fry, turning once, until golden brown and cooked through, 2 to 4 minutes. Transfer to a paper towel–lined plate. Season with salt.

5. Serve with lemon wedges, Chimichurri, Mignonette, prepared tartar sauce, hot sauce, and malt vinegar.

Chimichurri

Combine ½ cup finely chopped **fresh flat-leaf parsley,** ¼ cup **white wine vinegar,** 2 tablespoons **olive oil,** 2 cloves chopped **garlic,** 1 seeded and chopped **jalapeño,** and 1 tablespoon chopped **fresh oregano** in a bowl. Season with **kosher salt.** *Makes ⅔ cup.*

Mignonette

Combine ½ cup **red wine vinegar** and 1 small, finely chopped **shallot** in a bowl. Season with **kosher salt** and freshly **ground black pepper.** Let sit at least 30 minutes or up to 24 hours. *Makes ½ cup.*

Blackberry-Almond buckle

CATCH A DRIFT
Create thematic food markers with pieces of driftwood and a white paint pen.

Blackberry-Almond Buckle

Not to be confused with a biscuit-based cobbler, a buckle is a single-layer cake with berries or fruit in the batter, giving the end result a "buckled" appearance.

MAKES *8 to 10 servings*   **WORKING TIME** *40 minutes*   **TOTAL TIME** *1 hour 45 minutes*

FOR THE STREUSEL

- ½ **cup sugar**
- ½ **cup all-purpose flour, spooned and leveled**
- ½ **cup almond meal**
- ½ **teaspoon kosher salt**
- 4 **tablespoons (½ stick) unsalted butter, cut into pieces**

FOR THE CAKE

- ½ **cup (1 stick) unsalted butter, at room temperature, plus more for pan**
- 1 **cup all-purpose flour, spooned and leveled**
- ¾ **cup almond meal**
- 1 **teaspoon baking powder**
- ½ **teaspoon kosher salt**
- ¼ **teaspoon baking soda**
- 1 **cup sugar**
- 2 **large eggs**
- ½ **cup crème fraîche, plus more for serving**
- 10 **ounces (about 2½ cups) fresh blackberries**

1. Make the streusel: Preheat oven to 350°F. Whisk together sugar, flour, almond meal, and salt in a bowl. Using a fork or pastry blender, work in butter until mixture is crumbly. Refrigerate until ready to use.

2. Make the cake: Butter a 9-inch-round by 2-inch-deep cake pan and line the bottom with parchment paper.

3. Whisk together flour, almond meal, baking powder, salt, and baking soda in a bowl. Beat butter and sugar with an electric mixer on medium speed until light and fluffy, 3 to 4 minutes. Add eggs, one at a time, beating to incorporate after each addition and scraping down bowl as necessary. Reduce mixer speed to low and beat in flour mixture and crème fraîche alternately, beginning and ending with flour mixture, just until flour is incorporated.

4. Transfer batter to prepared pan. Top with blackberries and streusel. Bake until a toothpick inserted in the center comes out clean, 60 to 70 minutes. Let cool slightly.

5. Serve with crème fraîche alongside.

Know-How
SKIPPING A ROCK

Consider this your party trick for summer days spent lakeside. First, find a smooth, flat stone. The ideal skipping stone should be about the size of your palm and should feel slightly heavy. Place the stone in the crook of your index finger, with your thumb resting lightly on the flat top. Raise your hand, then swing out and down until the stone is at a 20-degree angle to the water. Release the stone forcefully, sending the stone spinning out, skimming the surface of the water.

· SUMMER ·

In the Garden

—◇—

*"Part of creating is understanding that there is always
more to do; nothing is ever completely finished."*
—Style icon and longtime Virginia resident Rachel Lambert "Bunny" Mellon

Blue, pink,
or purple?

The Southern Checklist

Hedge Your Bets with Hydrangea

····◇····

Stop and Smell the Gardenias

...and more
summer flowers
we love!

····◇····

Know Your Garden Tomatoes

····◇····

Become
a Brandywine
connoisseur.

Display Your Cosmos

HEDGE YOUR BETS WITH HYDRANGEA

There's a certain effortless, not-trying-too-hardness to the hydrangea. At home everywhere from the Mid-Atlantic to the Deep South, these three-season flowering shrubs, including the French mophead (above), make lush and loose garden hedges.

"I love their easygoing look," says Georgia-based landscape designer Carmen Johnston. "The cone-shaped oakleaf is my favorite for the way the flowers fade from white to weathered pink in the warm sun—just like perfectly worn cushions on a porch glider."

Stop and Smell the...

Gardenia

Gardenia jasminoides

WHY WE LOVE THEM
This perfumy evergreen plant is as elegant and hardy as *Designing Women*'s Julia Sugarbaker.

WHAT TO KNOW
Available in white, cream, or yellow, the humidity-loving perennial shrub can grow up to 8 feet tall.

FAVORITE VARIETIES
August Beauty, Fortuniana, Mystery, Frost Proof

Crepe Myrtle

Lagerstroemia indica

WHY WE LOVE IT
This popular ornamental tree thrives in the heat and humidity of the region.

WHAT TO KNOW
Before committing, be sure to research the plant's mature size, as varieties can range from 3 to 30 feet tall. (When Southerners prune the tall ones back to stubs, it's often called "crepe murder.")

FAVORITE VARIETIES
Queen's Crepe Myrtle, Catawba, Velma's Royal Delight

Common Honeysuckle

Lonicera periclymenum

WHY WE LOVE IT
The hardy flowering vine has a sweet fragrance, and its tubular flowers attract bees, butterflies, and hummingbirds.

WHAT TO KNOW
Common honeysuckle is not to be confused with invasive Japanese honeysuckle, which can grow well beyond 100 feet.

FAVORITE VARIETIES
Peaches and Cream, Sweet Tea, Scentsation

Zinnia

Zinnia elegans

WHY WE LOVE THEM
These easygoing annuals are beloved for their vibrant, bouquet-friendly blooms.

WHAT TO KNOW
Zinnias come in three kinds: single, semidouble, or double, which is based on the number of rows of petals and whether the flower's center is visible.

FAVORITE VARIETIES
Benary Giant, Magellan, Oklahoma, South of the Border, Queen Red Lime

FOR THE LOVE OF...

Late-Summer Gardens

Some Southern gardens take pride in their exactness: Think meticulously sculptured hedges, satisfyingly symmetrical plantings, precise paths. And then there's the late-summer cottage garden. If the formal garden is a realist painting, the cottage garden is more abstract, with misplaced thrivers and blurred borders. Unapologetically ebullient, this slightly mad, mostly magical mix reaches peak pandemonium when the lazy days of summer creep in like a wayward vine—when gardeners loosen their grip on the pruning shears in the name of, say, a vacation or full-blast AC. If that sounds like you, resist the urge to get to work and spend a moment immersed in the happy chaos, a reminder that, despite our best-laid plans, life goes on—and sometimes plants need to let loose, too.

Know Your Garden Tomatoes

Grown in 86 percent of home gardens, tomatoes are by far the most popular summer fruit to plant for the Southern set. Whether you are a master gardener with years of crop experience or an optimistic newbie putting your first plants in the ground, these varieties are worth keeping on the radar. (Word to the wise: Tomato sandwich enthusiasts should opt for Cherokee Purple or Brandywines.) And, as always, be sure to check with your local cooperative extension to find out what grows best in your specific area.

TINY TIM
An ideal cultivar for a container garden, this plant produces bundles of tiny red tomatoes and grows only 12 to 16 inches tall. It can even tolerate a little shade.

BRANDYWINE
One of the most popular home cultivars, these can grow up to 1½ pounds and are cherished for their sweet taste and acidity.

SUNGOLD
This prolific early ripener produces small, super-sweet fruit with a golden orange hue. The plant can grow up to 12 feet tall, so be prepared to stake it.

CHEROKEE PURPLE
Dusty pink to purple on the outside with a deep red interior, these large slicers have a sweet and rich, almost smoky flavor.

SUPER SWEET 100
The fruit-bearing stems of this hybrid variety can hold up to 100 über-sweet tomatoes each.

GREEN GIANT
This award-winner can produce fruit up to 32 ounces. Sweet-and-tangy green-and-yellow flesh makes it a real looker in a salad.

DISPLAY YOUR COSMOS

....

This easy-to-grow annual attracts pollinators like bees
and butterflies and adds cheer to summer gardens with petals
that come in a variety of vivid colors. Pair with chamomile
in a vintage battery jar for a sweet-and-simple arrangement.

From the Kitchen

*"It's difficult to think anything but pleasant
thoughts while eating a homegrown tomato."*
—Author and Georgia native Lewis Grizzard

The Southern Checklist

Make Pimento Cheese Dip

· ◇ ·

Dish Out a Fresh Tomato Pie

· ◇ ·

Try Cheerwine Ribs

Just trust us on this.

· ◇ ·

Grill a Peach-and-Bacon Pizza

· ◇ ·

Serve a Key Lime Slab Pie

It's a Jimmy Buffett song in food form.

Keep 'em Appetized

Pimento Cheese Dip

———— ◦ ————

There's a reason this crowd-pleaser is known as "the caviar of the South." Give this recipe your own signature twist by mixing up the cheeses—freshly grated Monterey Jack Gouda, or Havarti—and by adding herbs, dried spices, roasted Hatch chiles, or different mustards. You can eat this right away, but a little rest in the fridge helps all the flavors meld.

WORKING TIME *15 minutes*   **TOTAL TIME** *8 hours*   **MAKES** *3½ cups*

⅓ cup **mayonnaise**

1 **(4-ounce) jar diced pimentos,** drained

1 large **scallion,** chopped

2 teaspoons **Dijon mustard**

Dash **Worcestershire sauce**

Dash **hot sauce**

1 pound **cheese** (such as sharp Cheddar, Monterey Jack, Gouda, or Havarti), grated (about 4 cups)

Kosher salt and freshly ground **black pepper**

Quick Summer Pickles, recipe following, and crostini, for serving

1. Beat mayonnaise, pimentos, scallion, mustard, Worcestershire, and hot sauce with an electric mixture on low speed until combined, about 1 minute.

2. With mixer running, slowly add cheese in three additions. Mix just until evenly combined and some of the cheese has broken down, 1 to 2 minutes. Season with salt and pepper. Cover and chill overnight. Serve with Quick Summer Pickles and crostini alongside.

Quick Summer Pickles

Place 1½ cups **mixed summer vegetables** in a heatproof bowl or 2-quart glass jar with a tight-fitting lid. Cook 2 cups **unseasoned rice wine vinegar,** 5 tablespoons **sugar,** 2 tablespoons **kosher salt,** 3 cloves smashed **garlic,** 1 **fresh bay leaf,** 1½ teaspoons each **fennel seeds** and **mustard seeds,** ½ teaspoon **black peppercorns,** ¼ teaspoon **red pepper flakes,** and 2 cups **water** in a medium saucepan over medium heat until sugar is dissolved. Pour over vegetables. Let stand until cool, about 1 hour. Cover and chill at least 24 hours.

A SHORT HISTORY OF...

The Masters Pimento Cheese Sandwiches

Anyone familiar with the esteemed Georgia golf tournament knows that the Southern spread is as integral to the experience as the green jackets and azaleas. It was Nick Rangos, a caterer from Aiken, South Carolina, who first supplied the event with his signature (and still secret) recipe and did so for 40 years. However, in 1998, the tournament changed vendors, much to the chagrin of the dip's devotees. Now, the $1.50 sandwich is made in-house, but some who still crave the original insist the closest you can come is a recipe from a 2005 cookbook by the Junior League of Augusta.

Raid the Garden
Tomato Pie

———— ◇ ————

For the prettiest results, use a variety of yellow, red, and cherry or grape tomatoes.

WORKING TIME *1 hour 30 minutes* **TOTAL TIME** *4 hours 30 minutes (including chilling and cooling)*
MAKES *6 to 8 servings*

1¼ cups all-purpose flour, spooned and leveled, plus more for work surface

½ teaspoon kosher salt, plus more for seasoning

1 teaspoon sugar, divided

½ cup (1 stick) cold unsalted butter, cut into pieces, plus 1 tablespoon, divided

2 tablespoons ice-cold water and more if needed

½ large sweet onion, sliced

¼ teaspoon baking soda

1½ pounds assorted ripe tomatoes, divided

Freshly ground black pepper

1 teaspoon fresh thyme

1 teaspoon olive oil

2½ tablespoons fresh basil, chopped

8 slices bacon, cooked and roughly chopped

½ cup mayonnaise

1½ ounces grated Parmesan (about ⅓ cup)

1½ ounces grated Asiago (about ⅓ cup)

1. Whisk together flour, salt, and ½ teaspoon sugar in a bowl. Cut in ½ cup butter with two forks or a pastry blender until mixture resembles coarse meal with several pea-size pieces of butter remaining. Add water, one tablespoon at a time, using a fork to pull dough together into a crumbly pile. (Add an additional tablespoon of water, if needed.) Transfer dough to a large piece of plastic wrap. Use the plastic to flatten and press dough into a disc. Refrigerate until firm, 2 hours or overnight.

2. Preheat oven to 400°F. On a lightly floured work surface, roll pie dough into a 12-inch round. Fit dough in a 9-inch pie pan. Trim edges to 1 inch, turn overhang under, and crimp. Line dough with a large piece of parchment paper and fill with pie weights, dried beans, or rice. Bake until edges are set, about 30 minutes. Carefully remove pie weights and let crust cool completely on a wire rack.

2. Reduce oven to 375°F. Melt remaining tablespoon butter in a medium saucepan over medium-low heat. Add onion and baking soda. Cook, stirring occasionally, until golden brown, 14 to 16 minutes.

3. Chop half the tomatoes into ½-inch pieces. In a colander, toss chopped tomatoes with the remaining sugar and season with salt; let sit, about 30 minutes. Thinly slice remaining tomatoes and place in a single layer on a rimmed baking sheet. Sprinkle with thyme, oil, and more salt. Roast until slightly dried and starting to wrinkle, 25 to 30 minutes.

4. Reserve 3 to 4 sliced roasted tomatoes. Combine onions, both batches of tomatoes, basil, and bacon in a bowl. Stir together mayonnaise, Parmesan, and Asiago in a second bowl. Spoon tomato mixture into prebaked piecrust. Top with mayonnaise mixture and reserved tomatoes. Season with pepper.

5. Bake until cooked through and golden brown in center, 25 to 30 minutes, shielding edges of crust halfway through, if necessary. Serve warm or at room temperature.

Try a Twist on a Classic

Cheerwine Ribs

———◇———

The iconic Southern soda lends the perfect zing of sweetness to a
backyard cookout staple. In fact, the beverage pairs so well with BBQ that the
National Barbecue Association named Cheerwine its official drink.

MAKES *6 to 8 servings* **PREP TIME** *30 minutes* **TOTAL TIME** *3 hours 30 minutes*

- 2 **teaspoons smoked paprika**
- 2 **teaspoons chili powder**
- 2 **teaspoons mustard powder**
- 1 **teaspoon garlic powder**
- 1 **teaspoon ground ginger**
- **Kosher salt and freshly ground black pepper**
- 2 **(3-pound) slabs baby back ribs**
- 1 **(12-ounce) bottle Cheerwine**
- 1 **(15-ounce) can tomato sauce**
- ⅓ **cup light brown sugar**
- 1 **tablespoon Dijon mustard**
- 2 **teaspoons chili-garlic sauce**
- **Canola oil, for grill grates**

1. Preheat oven to 325°F. Stir together paprika, chili powder, mustard powder, garlic powder, ginger, 4 teaspoons salt, and 2 teaspoons pepper in bowl. Sprinkle 2 tablespoons spice mixture over ribs, dividing evenly. Place ribs on a rimmed baking sheet; wrap tightly with aluminum foil. Bake until tender, 2 to 2½ hours. Remove foil; let rest 30 minutes.

2. Combine Cheerwine, tomato sauce, brown sugar, Dijon mustard, chili-garlic sauce, and 1 tablespoon spice mixture in a medium saucepan. Bring to a boil over high heat. Reduce heat and simmer, stirring occasionally, until reduced to 2 cups, 25 to 30 minutes.

3. Heat grill to medium. Once hot, clean and oil grill grates. Grill ribs, basting with 1 cup of Cheerwine sauce and turning frequently, until lightly charred and lacquered, 10 to 15 minutes.

4. Transfer to a platter and serve with remaining Cheerwine sauce and spice mixture.

A SHORT HISTORY OF...
Cheerwine Soda

While there's no shortage of beloved Southern sodas (see page 111), Cheerwine, aka the "Nectar of North Carolina," has held a special place in Southerners' hearts for 100-plus years. The concoction dates to 1917, when, during a wartime sugar shortage, beverage maker L.D. Peeler set out to create a less sugary soda using a cherry flavoring he purchased from a St. Louis traveling salesman. Given its cheery disposition and burgundy-red color, L.D. named his invention Cheerwine, and the brand has remained in the family—and in the same small town of Salisbury—ever since. (Get your fizz fix at the annual Cheerwine Festival, which takes place in Salisbury every May.)

Fire Up the Grill

Peach-and-Bacon Pizza

———◇———

Southerners can't claim the culinary triumph that is pizza, although it was invented in *Southern* Italy. Still, when you add bacon and peak summer peaches, it bridges the best of both worlds.

WORKING TIME *30 minutes* **TOTAL TIME** *45 minutes* **MAKES** *4 servings*

Cornmeal, for baking sheet

All-purpose flour, for work surface

1 **pound store-bought pizza dough, at room temperature**

1 **cup whole-milk ricotta cheese**

Kosher salt and freshly ground black pepper

5 **slices thick-cut bacon, cooked and roughly chopped**

2 **medium peaches, sliced**

⅓ **cup Pickled Red Onions, recipe following**

1 **tablespoon pure honey**

1½ **tablespoons olive oil**

¼ **cup fresh basil**

1. Preheat oven to 475°F. Sprinkle a baking sheet with cornmeal or line with parchment paper. On a lightly floured work surface, shape pizza dough into a 12- by 10-inch rectangle and transfer to prepared baking sheet. Spread ricotta on dough, leaving a ¾-inch border all around. Season with salt and pepper. Top with bacon, peaches, and Pickled Red Onions. Drizzle with honey and oil.

2. Bake until crust is deep golden brown, 15 to 17 minutes. Top with basil. Serve immediately.

Pickled Red Onions

Cook ½ cup **champagne vinegar,** 1 tablespoon **sugar,** and ½ teaspoon **black peppercorns** in a small saucepan over medium heat until sugar is dissolved, about 1 minute. Add 1 cup thinly sliced **red onion,** and cook 1 minute. Cool completely. *Makes about ½ cup.*

A SHORT HISTORY OF...

Key Lime Pie

Before the 1938 opening of the 113-mile Overseas Highway through the Florida Keys to Key West, fresh milk was tough to come by in the hard-to-access Keys, making canned sweetened condensed milk a staple of this regional dish. There's still debate among Floridians about the ideal crust— this one is a buttery pastry; others call for graham—but most agree that green food coloring is a big no-no.

Brake for Pie
Key Lime Slab Pie

———◇———

This refreshing citrusy staple is the next best thing to strolling the pastel-hued streets of Key West.

WORKING TIME *30 minutes*　**TOTAL TIME** *8 hours 20 minutes (includes chilling)*　**MAKES** *12 servings*

FOR THE PIE DOUGH

- 2½ cups all-purpose flour, spooned and leveled, plus more for work surface
- 1 teaspoon kosher salt
- 1 teaspoon sugar
- 1 cup (2 sticks) cold unsalted butter, cut into pieces
- ¼ cup ice-cold water

FOR THE FILLING

- 2 (14-ounce) cans sweetened condensed milk
- 8 large egg yolks
- Zest plus fresh juice from key limes (or regular limes), about 1½ tablespoons zest and 1½ cups juice
- ¼ teaspoon kosher salt

FOR THE TOPPING

- 2 cups heavy cream
- ¼ cup confectioners' sugar
- Candied Lime Zest, recipe following

1. Whisk together flour, salt, and sugar in a bowl. Cut in butter with two forks or a pastry blender until mixture resembles coarse meal with several pea-size pieces of butter remaining. Add 2 tablespoons water, 1 tablespoon at a time, using a fork to pull dough together into a crumbly pile. (Add up to an additional 2 tablespoons of water, if needed.) Transfer dough to a large piece of plastic wrap. Use the plastic to flatten and press dough into a disc. Refrigerate until firm, 2 hours or overnight.

1. Preheat oven to 375°F with racks in lowest and middle positions. On a lightly floured work surface, roll dough to an 18- by 13-inch rectangle. Fit dough into a 15- by 10-inch jelly-roll pan, fold edges under, and crimp. Prick bottom of dough several times with a fork; freeze 20 minutes. Line dough with a large piece of parchment paper and fill with pie weights, dried beans, or rice. Bake, on bottom rack, 18 to 20 minutes. Carefully remove parchment paper and pie weights. Bake until light golden brown, 12 to 15 minutes. Cool completely on a wire rack.

2. Make the filling: Reduce oven temperature to 325°F. Whisk together condensed milk, egg yolks, lime zest and juice, and salt in a bowl. Pour into prebaked piecrust. Bake, on middle rack, until edges are set and center jiggles only slightly, 14 to 16 minutes. Cool to room temperature, then chill at least 3 hours or up to overnight.

3. Make the topping: Beat together cream and confectioners' sugar with an electric mixer on medium-high speed until soft peaks form, about 30 seconds. Spoon on top of pie and top with lime zest.

Candied Lime Zest

Line a rimmed baking sheet with parchment paper. Cut the peel from 3 large **limes** into ¼-inch-wide strips. Place peel in a medium saucepan and cover with water. Bring to a boil and cook until tender, 8 to 10 minutes. Transfer to a wire rack to drain. Combine blanched lime peel, ½ cup **granulated sugar,** and ½ cup **water** in a small saucepan. Bring to a boil over medium-high heat. Reduce heat and simmer until liquid is slightly thickened and peel is translucent, 6 to 8 minutes. Place ⅓ cup **sanding sugar** in a bowl. Add cooked peel and toss to coat; place on prepared baking sheet. Let stand until dry, 25 to 30 minutes. *Makes about ¾ cup*

· SUMMER ·

On the Go

———◆———

"Summer in the Deep South is not only a season, a climate, it's a dimension. Floating in it, one must be either proud or submerged."
—Writer and Alabama native Eugene Walter

The Southern Checklist

Explore Apalachicola, Florida

····◆····

It's Old Florida at its salty finest.

Visit a Southern Soda Fountain

····◆····

Go Antiquing for Canning Jars

◆ **PLUS** ◆

So many uses, so little time!

More Southern Wit & Wisdom

INDULGE YOUR YONDERLUST

Apalachicola, Florida

First of all, it's just plain fun to say. *Ap-a-lach-i-cola.* (Country artist Tim McGraw even sings about the multisyllabic spot in his song "Southern Voice.") And, while much of Florida's Gulf Coast has gotten quite crowded in recent years, this oft-overlooked portion of the Panhandle happily maintains hidden-gem charm. (It's located along a 60-mile stretch of Highway 98 known as "Florida's Forgotten Coast.") The word "Apalach" means land of the friendly people, and you'll find that this quaint community is filled with just that, from jovial fishermen to friendly sales clerks. That hospitable spirit also extends to the centrally located Gibson Inn (above), which has charmed sun-kissed visitors since 1907. (The property's wraparound porches, wood-paneled Parlor Bar, and newly gussied-up guest rooms also help.)

ABOUT APALACHICOLA OYSTERS

A highly sought-after regional delicacy, these flat and plump oysters have a distinct flavor profile that's the result of the unique blend of salt and fresh water in the Apalachicola Bay. They're also part of the region's rich maritime history. Oysters were harvested and sold locally as early as the 1830s. By the early 1900s, there were several seafood dealers, and the county led the state in oyster production. In 2020, due to efforts to restore conditions in Apalachicola Bay, Florida imposed a moratorium on the wild oyster harvest through 2025.

Apalachicola

No. 1
Unspoiled Beaches
The nearby barrier island of St. George is the perfect place to dip your toes. History buffs can explore the Cape St. George lighthouse and museum.

No. 2
Coastal Curiosities
For giftables galore, head over to Riverside Mercantile. And don't forget to stop into Retsyo Inc., where proprietor John Lee will happily regale you with colorful local lore.

No. 3
Sea-Salted Charm
With more than 900 historic homes and buildings dating back to the 1830s, it's no wonder the antiquing around these parts is so good. Bring home a buoy, why don't you?

No. 4
Fresh Seafood
Despite the moratorium on harvesting (see left), you can still enjoy oysters grown through aquaculture farming. Pair them with a beer from local Oyster City Brewing Co.

More Small Towns to Explore in Summer

BREVARD, NORTH CAROLINA
Boasting more than 250 waterfalls, this mountain stop is also famous for white squirrels, fly-fishing, and a charming downtown.

ST. MICHAELS, MARYLAND
Less than two hours from D.C., this Chesapeake Bay town feels like an 1800s seaport thanks to redbrick sidewalks and historic architecture.

EUREKA SPRINGS, ARKANSAS
Tucked in the Ozark Mountains, this artsy and eccentric enclave lures visitors with its hiking and biking trails and storied healing waters.

Visit a Southern Soda Fountain

Southerners seem to know a thing or two about soda. After all, we invented Coca-Cola, Pepsi, Dr. Pepper, Mountain Dew, Cheerwine, and the list goes on (see right). Typically tucked into a local apothecary or drugstore, the Southern soda fountain symbolizes our love for bubbles—and for the banter. There's nothing like walking into a place where everyone knows your name and your order. "Our regulars are more than our friends—they're part of our family," says Don Trowbridge, owner of 100-year-old soda fountain Trowbridge's Diner in idyllic downtown Florence, Alabama. Don (above), who started cranking ice cream in the back as a young boy, finds his customers crave the familiar charms of the century-old operation. "It tickles me to see a grandmother and her granddaughter sitting at the counter, and the grandmother will say, 'Honey, my granny and I used to sit on these same two vinyl stools when I was your age.'"

More Soda Fountains Worth a Visit

Gruene General Store and Soda Fountain
New Braunfels, Texas

Established in 1878 and reopened in 1989, this old-fashioned emporium (left) offers coffee for a nickel and free samples of fudge.

Leopold's Ice Cream
Savannah, Georgia

Look for the pink neon sign of this century-old soda fountain, then place your order with the smiling employees in red bow ties.

Brent's Drugs
Jackson, Mississippi

Since 1946, this spot has been a Jackson institution. Come for the house-made cherry syrup, stay for the late-night cocktails at the Apothecary bar tucked in the back.

Elliston Place Soda Shop
Nashville, Tennessee

Fun fact: In 1976, George Jones featured this Music City mainstay on his *Alone Again* album cover.

MORE SOUTHERN SODAS TO KNOW

Nehi
The name of this soda, invented in 1924 by Georgia businessman Claud Hatcher, refers to the tall ("knee-high") bottle height.

Grapico
Introduced in 1916 in New Orleans by J. Grossman's Sons, this grape-flavored sparkling soda is now bottled by Buffalo Rock in Birmingham, Alabama.

Barq's
While the company was founded in New Orleans in 1890, it wasn't until 1898, when Edward Barq moved to Biloxi, Mississippi, that the root beer came to be.

Collect Vintage Canning Jars

During the 1840s to the 1920s, hundreds of glassware companies were vying for a spot on America's shelves. And while Southerners can't fully claim the most iconic—that would be the Ball mason jar, which can be traced to Buffalo, followed by Muncie, Indiana—it became a household staple in the region for storing fruits and vegetables in the days before refrigeration. Here are a few of the more collectible styles that were frequently used for "puttin' up" seasonal produce.

NO. 1
Upside-Down Jar

Issued by **Ball** only from 1900 to 1910, this jar could double as a dispenser for a coffee grinder. The short production window gives it considerable cachet. **VALUE:** $1,000

NO. 2
Violet Jar

Manganese in these jars by **Columbia** created a purple tint when exposed to the sun. The color was initially an error, but manufacturers began selling the shade in 1905. **VALUE:** $400

NO. 3
Lightning Jar

In the common green shade, this wire bale 1910 model by **Ball** commands a respectable rate. A rare cobalt blue model fetches $10,000 or more. **VALUE:** $400

NO. 4
Sun Jar

This 1890s **Bartow** style was known for its lever tops. Buyer beware: Reproductions abound. If a lid's metal looks pristine, it's likely too good to be true. **VALUE:** $175

SUMMER WIT & WISDOM

More ways to embrace the season in the swelter.

NEIGHBORLY NICETIES

Become the Welcome Wagon

Greet newcomers to the block with a happy handout and dossier on their new 'hood's best haunts.

THE GIFT A houseplant

THE GREETING "We're so happy you're laying down roots here."

THE GIFT Fresh bread from a nearby bakery

THE GREETING "Let us know if you knead anything."

THE GIFT A six-pack of Southern soda

THE GREETING "Soda-lighted you're our neighbor."

THE GIFT Punch fixin's

THE GREETING "We're pleased as punch to have you on our street."

BACKYARD BASICS
Hang a Tire Swing

First, you'll need a seat. A tire with at least a 17-inch inner diameter will make for a roomier ride. Next, find a sturdy branch—a maple or oak is a good bet—at least 10 inches in diameter and 7 to 9 feet from the ground. Wrap one end of 50 feet of braided polypropylene rope (at hardware stores) around the branch a few times, securing it with a fisherman's bend or bowline knot. Determine the swing height (typically 2 feet above ground), and wrap and knot the rope's end around the tire. Test, trim rope as needed, and swing away.

SOUNDTRACK

Compile a Playlist

Singer-songwriter Holly Audrey Williams shares her backroad repeats.

"Ramblin' Man"
by The Allman Brothers Band

"Back Down South"
by Kings of Leon

"Georgia on My Mind"
by Ray Charles

"The Eye"
by Brandi Carlile

"Walking in Memphis"
by Marc Cohn

"Mississippi"
by Sheryl Crow

"Traveling Alone"
by Jason Isbell

"Amazing Grace"
by the Blind Boys of Alabama

IDENTIFICATION KEY

Fireworks

How's this for a claim to flame: Missourians (reportedly) spend the most on pyrotechnics per capita than any other state.

Chrysanthemum

Palm

Spider

SUMMER HAPPENINGS

Whether you're into nature or knickknacks, there's something to wet your whistle.

Synchronous Fireflies Viewing
Great Smoky Mountains

You'll have to enter a lottery via the National Park Service for a chance to see this early-summer spectacle, when thousands of lightning bugs blink in sync.

RC Cola-MoonPie Festival
Bell Buckle, Tennessee

Every year, on the third Saturday of June, this central Tennessee town pays tribute to the South's original fast-food combo.

FloydFest
Floyd, Virginia

Held every July, this five-day music and arts festival in the Blue Ridge Mountains offers beer, bluegrass, and more mountain merriment.

127 Yard Sale
Alabama, Georgia, Tennessee, Kentucky

Known as "The World's Longest Yard Sale," this early August shopping event spans 690 miles and six states, four of which are Southern.

SOUTHERNISMS, EXPLAINED

"Hotter than Hinges"

Also uttered as "Hot as Hinges" or "Hot as the Hinges on the Gates of Hell," this expression refers to the brutal fiery heat experienced during the dog days of summer.

ONLY IN THE SOUTH...

SEED SPITTING WORLD CHAMPIONSHIP

At the annual Watermelon Thump festival in Luling, Texas, contestants get two spits to earn bragging rights. If you want a go, Texas-based spitting champ Davis Camacho says to shape your tongue like a taco, placing a large, heavy seed in the middle with the tapered end facing out. Then, use lung power to propel the seed down the "spit way." (The record is 75 feet, 2 inches!)

HOME REMEDY

Shucking Corn

Keep errant kernels at bay with this easy hack. First, hold a shucked corn cob upright on the center tube (or "funnel") of a Bundt or angel food pan. Then, using a chef's knife, remove the kernels by cutting from top to bottom, between the kernels and the cob. The kernels will fall into the pan. Remove kernels and enjoy!

Willow

Peony

Horsetail

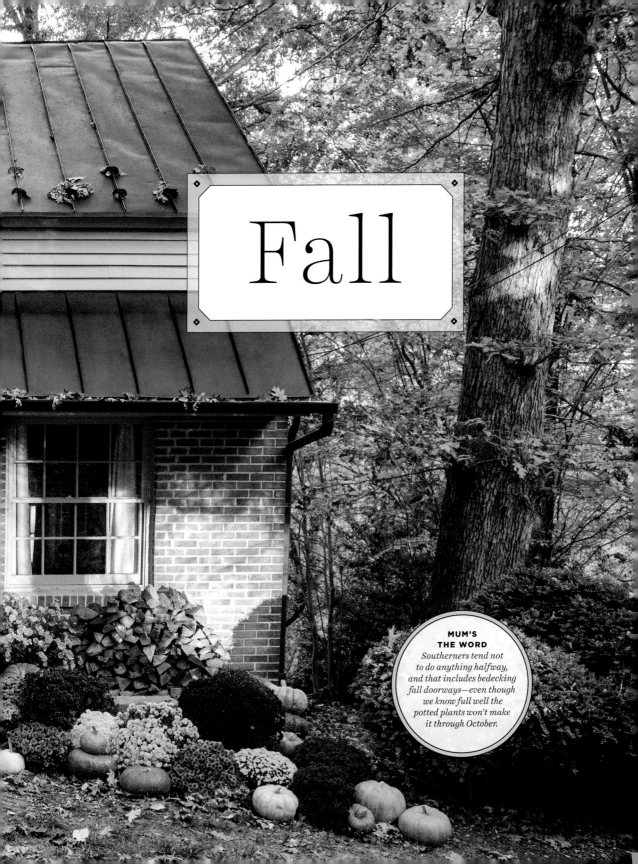

Fall

MUM'S THE WORD
Southerners tend not to do anything halfway, and that includes bedecking fall doorways—even though we know full well the potted plants won't make it through October.

It's Not *Fall* in the South Without...

·····◇·····

A trip to your favorite
mountain town, complete
with winding roads and
"See Rock City" signage

◇

Fancying up your
antique sideboard and
reflecting on the family
recipes that have graced
its surface over time

◇

The return of tailgating
season and all of the "thermos
cuisine" that goes with it

◇

Wondering if it's
too soon to buy
pumpkins because it's
still 90 degrees

◇

Settling in by the firepit
even though it still
feels a heckuva lot like
summer outside

◇

The circle of life that
is the Thanksgiving kids'
table and the sweet
overheard snippets of
cousin conversation

Around the House

> *"The ache for home lives in all of us. The safe place where we can go as we are and not be questioned."*
> —**Author and Missouri native Maya Angelou**

The Southern Checklist

Create a Cozy Porch

By Southern authors, naturally!

Pair a Nook with a Book

Embrace Mismatched Seating

Give new meaning to "face value."

Display an Oil Portrait

Put Your Plates on Display

Create a Cozy Porch

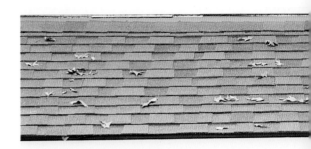

Although spring and summer tend to get all the porch-season glory, Southerners know that fall is truly the most prime of times to sit a spell. With crisper temperatures, vibrant foliage, and the faint smell of a fire burning somewhere in the distance, it's the year's golden hour—a season seemingly tailor-made for old-soul sorts who are content to rest and reminisce on a porch swing. There's nothing quite like staking out a spot to take in the seasonal spectacle while sipping an autumnal beverage (see right) and listening to game day on the radio.

As cozy as a porch party of one can be, autumn also marks the bustling fall-iday season, with a constant stream of revelers and relatives dropping by for everything from candy corn to candied yams. Whether you're swinging solo or welcoming visitors, here's how to put your best front forward.

NO. 1
Lush Leaves

Interwoven with dried bittersweet on the garland and basket, waxy magnolia leaves make for a gracious, deep-green welcome.

NO. 2
Rustic Swing

Embellished with dark hickory logs, a solid wood two-seater beckons bundling up under a blanket.

NO. 3
Basket Wreath

Used to bring the tobacco crop to market in 1800s North Carolina, these baskets also make for seasonal door swag.

NO. 4
Orange Crush

For an autumnal entry, nothing rivals an orange door (Pumpkin Patch by Glidden) flanked by gourds.

CIDER BOURBON PUNCH

Consider this the cocktail equivalent of your favorite flannel shirt. Cook four cups of **fresh apple cider** in a medium saucepan over medium-high heat until reduced to 1½ cups (about 30 minutes); cool completely. Transfer to a punch bowl or pitcher, then stir in 3 cups of **bourbon,** 15 shakes **Angostura bitters,** and ½ cup **freshly squeezed orange juice.** Stir in 2 cups of **seltzer.** Garnish with **apple slices.** Serve over ice garnished with **bourbon cherries.**

PAIR A NOOK WITH A BOOK

···

No. 1
RUSTIC RETREAT
This setting calls for a richly layered book to get lost in, like *Where the Line Bleeds* by Jesmyn Ward.

No. 2
LONE STAR LEISURE
Kick off those boots. This corner of a Texas farmhouse pairs well with *Lonesome Dove* by Larry McMurtry.

No. 3
MOUNTAIN MAGIC
This cozy spot calls for something set in Appalachia. Try *Demon Copperhead* by Barbara Kingsolver.

No. 4
CABIN COMFORT
With its bourbon-hued wood and rugged stool, this spot says Faulkner. Try *The Sound and the Fury*.

Go for Mismatched Seating

Pull up a chair. As families across the South convene this time of year, putting aside any grudges in the name of gravy, there's something sweetly symbolic about a dining table surrounded by seating of all stripes: a stately Windsor alongside a humble ladder-back positioned next to a 100-year-old high chair. A mix-and-match tableau offers a visual reminder that there's value in the varied—and always a way to accommodate a last-minute guest or two. After all, a family is a collection of sorts, and it's the quirks and imperfections—rather than the shared traits or common surname—that keep things interesting. As you approach the Thanksgiving season and beyond, let go of the "matching set" mindset. It's the perfect occasion to embrace a seating arrangement as delightfully disparate as the cast of characters who will soon populate the table.

WALL FLOWERS
Homeowner Lauren Northup hand-painted the walls of her South Carolina home with a Tree of Life stencil.

Display an Oil Portrait

Nothing adds personality to a room like a literal personality, whether it's in the form of a commissioned portrait or one found while antiquing. Southerners love storytelling, after all, and portraiture is another form of it. Aaron Beane, marketing director for Portraits, Inc., the world's oldest and largest commissioned portrait company, says that, while the company got its start in New York City 80-plus years ago, Southerners make up its largest customer base. (He also notes the company has seen record sales in recent years, which points to a growing desire for heirloom-worthy artwork in an increasingly ephemeral world.)

Of course, you don't have to spring for commissioned artwork. Antique oil portraits—think "acquired" ancestors— lend their own mystique to a space. For example, Nashville designer Stephanie Sabbe lucked upon this cotillion club–esque grouping, painted in the style of Nashville artist Lula B. Estes, at a local estate sale. (Estes's portraits depicted some of the movers and shakers of Music City society.)

PUT YOUR PLATES ON DISPLAY

No. 1
TRANSFERWARE
When arranged in
a wreath shape, a
classic collection takes
on new life above
a wooden huntboard.

No. 2
FEATHERED FRIENDS
Outfitted with both
plates and glassware, a
game-themed hutch
in the Mississippi Delta
is a lesson in fowl play.

No. 3
SPODE WOODLAND
Featuring pheasants and
deer, the autumnal
classic feels right at home
in a rustic yet refined
Alabama cabin.

No. 4
BLUE ONION
In West Virginia, a
plate rack showcases
a bevy of blue and
white, including this
cobalt-hued collectible.

At the Table

"Gratitude is a quality similar to electricity: It must be produced and discharged and used up in order to exist at all."
—Author and Mississippi native William Faulkner

Family photos encouraged.

The Southern Checklist

Set a Southern Thanksgiving Table

·····◇·····

Pick Your Place Setting

·····◇·····

Create a Seasonal Centerpiece

It's time to pull out the pewter.

·····◇·····

Host a Winning Game-Day Gathering

And win at cornhole while you're at it!

Set a Southern Thanksgiving Table

A warm and weathered farm table set with mismatched plates, hand-me-down linens, and silver collected over time is, quite fittingly, as beautifully hodgepodge as the people who will soon surround it. Using old family photos helps guests find their seats, but, more important, it helps inspire all sorts of "remember when" banter. "Objects are memory capsules—they unlock stories," says Marjorie Hunt, folklorist and curator for the Smithsonian Center for Folklife and Cultural Heritage. A simple question like, "Grandpa, who's that guy in the photo on your right?" will likely yield a wonderful anecdote. Marjorie also suggests recording the kitchen cacophony as the meal is prepared. It's one thing to write down family history—but nothing compares to capturing Grandma's thick-as-molasses accent on audio for posterity.

NO. 1
Mismatched Plates

Little brings soul to the setting quite like heirlooms (linens and flatware included!).

NO. 2
Woven Chargers

They add pretty texture and cohesion to a more collected tablescape.

NO. 3
Right-Height Arrangement

Keep your blooms below 16 inches tall so everyone stays within sight.

NO. 4
Photo Place Cards

For an old-timey feel, print them all out with a black-and-white or sepia filter.

PICK YOUR PLACE SETTING

No. 1
APPLE PICKIN'
A ruby red apple topped with a green paper-leaf place card tastefully invites guests to their seats.

No. 2
STICK TO IT
Tuck a place card into the natural crevice of a cinnamon stick, then wrap each end with red twine.

No. 3
BEST IN BOW
Fold a napkin into a long rectangle. Fold it again into thirds and slip on a gold napkin ring. Pull out ends to make the tails.

No. 4
SPOON FED
For a more rustic approach, use a vintage wooden spoon as a place card, and create a napkin ring with nuts.

Create a
Seasonal Centerpiece

Prized for their unique shape and medicinal properties, Chinese lanterns grow with vigor in full sun and take on an orange hue come autumn. For an arrangement that celebrates the season, combine the stems with leafy branches and fluffy marigolds in a passed-down pewter pitcher.

Host a Winning Game-Day Gathering

When the season's social calendar revolves around kickoff,
you know football is serious business*. Here's how to serve up a spirited
assortment of fan fare, whether you're at home or away.

*For pure objectivity purposes, no SEC logos were used in this setup. (We wouldn't dare take sides!)

STUB HUB
*Corral school ephemera
(old ticket stubs, photos)
beneath a piece of glass or
plexiglass set into a serving
tray. (Many hardware
stores will cut glass to your
dimensions.)*

Smoky Slow Cooker Beef Tacos and Fixin's

It's simply not game day without something simmering in a slow cooker. Oh, and guacamole.

WORKING TIME *15 minutes*   **TOTAL TIME** *5 hours 15 minutes or 8 hours 15 minutes*   **MAKES** *8 servings*

1 (8-ounce) can tomato sauce

1 tablespoon chopped chipotle in adobo, plus 1 tablespoon adobo sauce

2 teaspoons ground cumin

4 cloves garlic, pressed

1 red onion, thinly sliced

1¾ pounds flank steak, cut crosswise against the grain into 2½-inch-wide pieces

Kosher salt

Corn tortillas, sour cream, and pico de gallo, for serving

Pepita Guacamole and Black Bean-and-Pineapple Salad, for serving, recipes following

1. Combine tomato sauce, chipotle, adobo sauce, and cumin in a 5- to 6-quart slow cooker. Stir in garlic, onion, and steak. Season with salt. Cover and cook until meat is very tender, 4 to 5 hours on high or 7 to 8 hours on low. Shred beef with two forks.

2. Serve with tortillas, sour cream, pico de gallo, Pepita Guacamole, and Black Bean-and-Pineapple Salad alongside.

Pepita Guacamole

Combine 3 large **avocados,** ¼ cup finely diced **white onion,** 3 tablespoons chopped fresh **cilantro,** 1 small finely chopped **jalapeño,** ¼ cup finely chopped **roasted pepitas,** and 4 tablespoons **fresh lime juice** in a bowl. Mash with a fork until combined and avocado is desired consistency. Season with **salt** and **pepper.** Top with additional **pepitas.** *Makes 8 servings.*

Black Bean-and-Pineapple Salad

Combine ¼ cup **fresh lime juice,** 1 thinly sliced **jalapeño,** and ¼ thinly sliced small **red onion** in a bowl. Let sit, tossing occasionally, until onion begins to soften, 8 to 10 minutes. Add 2½ cups chopped **pineapple,** 2 (15-ounce) cans **black beans** (rinsed), and ½ cup chopped **fresh cilantro;** toss to combine. Top with **cotija cheese** before serving.

Cajun Sausage Puffs
with Bourbon Mustard

This crowd-pleasing twist on pigs in a blanket is a touchdown in tailgate form.
(And the mustard has a dash of bourbon to boot!)

WORKING TIME *25 minutes* **TOTAL TIME** *55 minutes (plus chilling)* **MAKES** *8 servings*

All-purpose flour, for work surface

½ (17.2-ounce) package frozen all-butter puff pastry, thawed

8 fully cooked andouille sausages

½ cup whole-grain Dijon mustard

1 tablespoon honey

2 teaspoons bourbon

1 large egg, whisked

1. Lightly dust work surface with flour. Unfold pastry onto floured surface; lightly flour top. Cut pastry crosswise into 16 (½-inch-wide) strips with a large chef's knife or pizza wheel.

2. Working one at a time, spiral strips around sausage (pushing the ends of a new strip into the old strip when you come to the end) until sausage is covered. Repeat with remaining strips and sausages. Chill 1 hour and up to 2 days.

3. Meanwhile, combine mustard, honey, and bourbon in a bowl.

4. Preheat the oven to 375°F. Brush pastry with egg. Bake until puffed and golden brown, 22 to 25 minutes. Cool 5 minutes, and then slice into 1-inch pieces with a serrated knife. Serve with mustard sauce alongside.

FOR THE LOVE OF...
The Magic City Classic

If you know, you *know.* Played annually at Legion Field in Birmingham, Alabama, since 1940, this October showdown between Alabama A&M University and Alabama State University is the largest historically Black college and university football game in the country, with a stadium attendance that exceeds 60,000 and an estimated 140,000 more who come just for the parades, pep rallies, and tailgates. If you are lucky enough to score a ticket to the game, don't hit up concessions during halftime because the competition is just as fierce during the battle of the bands between A&M's Marching Maroon & White and ASU's Mighty Marching Hornets.

Football Whoopie Pies with Cinnamon Cream

With these pigskin-inspired sandwiches, even the smack talk-iest
of rivals won't be able to argue against your game-day dessert dominance.

WORKING TIME *1 hour*   **TOTAL TIME** *2 hours*   **MAKES** *14 sandwiches*

FOR THE CAKE

- 2¼ **cups all-purpose flour, spooned and leveled**
- ¾ **cup Dutch-processed cocoa powder**
- ¾ **teaspoon baking soda**
- ½ **teaspoon baking powder**
- ½ **teaspoon kosher salt**
- ½ **cup (1 stick) unsalted butter, at room temperature**
- 1 **cup packed brown sugar**
- 1 **large egg, at room temperature**
- 1 **teaspoon pure vanilla extract**
- 1 **cup buttermilk, at room temperature**

FOR THE FILLING

- ½ **cup (1 stick) unsalted butter, at room temperature**
- 1⅔ **cups confectioners' sugar**
- ¼ **teaspoon ground cinnamon**

Pinch kosher salt

Store-bought white decorating icing

1. Make the cake: Preheat the oven to 400°F. Line two large baking sheets with parchment paper.

2. Whisk together flour, cocoa powder, baking soda, baking powder, and salt in a bowl. Beat butter and brown sugar on medium-high speed with an electric mixer until light and fluffy, 3 to 4 minutes. Reduce mixer speed to medium and beat in egg and vanilla until combined. Reduce mixer speed to low and beat in flour mixture and buttermilk alternately, beginning and ending with flour mixture, just until flour is incorporated. Transfer to a piping bag or a large zip-top bag with a ½-inch hole cut in one corner.

3. Pipe footballs onto prepared baking sheets by drawing 2½-inch football shapes on parchment paper, spacing 2 inches apart; invert paper. Following the outline, pipe from one end of the football, along the outer edge, and to the other end. Repeat along the opposite edge. Fill center of football. Smooth top with a small offset spatula or your finger. Bake, in batches, until puffed and just set, 6 to 7 minutes. Transfer to wire racks to cool.

4. Make the filling: Beat butter on medium speed with an electric mixer until pale, 4 to 5 minutes. Reduce mixer speed to low and add half the confectioners' sugar, beating until just incorporated. Add remaining sugar, cinnamon, and salt and continue beating until fluffy, 1 to 2 minutes.

5. Spoon filling onto flat sides of half of whoopie pies and sandwich together with unfrosted halves. Use icing to pipe football laces on top.

Know-How

CONQUERING CORNHOLE

Perfect your beanbag toss with tips from the pros at the American Cornhole Association. First, find a comfortable stance and relax. Aim your beanbag for the first six inches of the board, not the hole. Momentum will likely take your bag farther than you think. Throw it like a Frisbee, flat with an even, consistent spin to improve power and accuracy. After mastering these basics, you're well equipped for an "air mail" shot (the cornhole equivalent of a hole in one).

· FALL ·

In the Garden

———◇———

*"Autumn was her happiest season. There
was an expectancy about its sound and shapes."*
—Author and Alabama native Harper Lee

The Southern Checklist

Hang a Pretty Basket

·····◇·····

Your porch
will thank you.

Warm Up Your Welcome

·····◇·····

Make room for
the Neighborhood
Beautification
Award!

Display Your Dahlias

·····◇·····

Stop and Smell the Marigolds

...and more fall
flowers we love!

Hang a Pretty Basket

◦

Line your vessel (here, a round zinc orb) with sheet moss,
then fill it with soil and dried angel vine, which, like a flower frog,
helps hold things in place. From there, anything goes! Add annuals,
succulents, cut branches, or pumpkins for a boost of color.

WARM UP YOUR WELCOME

No. 1
LUSH & LEAFY
A garland of dried hydrangea and foliage alongside demijohns brings tons of texture.

No. 2
MAD FOR PLAID
Etched plaid pumpkins, mums in galvanized buckets, and bold branches make for a farmhouse-fresh scheme.

No. 3
CROCK PARTY
Vintage butter crocks come in handy for stacked displays, while also adding country charm.

No. 4
FEELING BATTY
Spooky-inclined sorts can opt for a mossy wreath, nailhead pumpkins, and brooms on each window.

DISPLAY YOUR DAHLIAS

These sun-loving stems grow in a range of warm shades, including the maroon Night Butterfly and orange Melody Dora. It's no wonder they're a preferred pick for fall arrangements, as shown here using an antique biscuit barrel as the vessel.

Stop and Smell the...

Marigold
Tagetes erecta

WHY WE LOVE THEM
Marigolds are the perfect choice to add autumn color in the still-hot South because they tolerate heat and humidity. They also repel pests, keeping gardens healthy and front-porch guests happy.

WHAT TO KNOW
These sun-loving blooms are low-maintenance and bloom well into fall, providing vibrant color when other flowers are fading.

FAVORITE VARIETIES
Moonsong Deep Orange, African Marigold, Mexican Tarragon

Pansy
Viola × wittrockiana

WHY WE LOVE THEM
Pansies thrive in the cooler temperatures of fall and even early winter. They provide a burst of color when other plants are dormant and can bloom for months, often lasting from fall through spring.

WHAT TO KNOW
Their colorful blooms and compact size make them ideal for borders, containers, and hanging baskets.

FAVORITE VARIETIES
Purple Rain, Monkey Face, Ballerina

Goldenrod
Solidago

WHY WE LOVE THEM
With their cheerful yellow clusters, these low-maintenance beauties pop up on roadsides and in garden beds every autumn. They can even handle occasional heat waves and poor soil.

WHAT TO KNOW
Goldenrod is also a crucial source of nectar for bees, butterflies, and other important pollinators.

FAVORITE VARIETIES
Fireworks, Golden Fleece, Crown of Rays

Petunia
Petunia × atkinsiana

WHY WE LOVE THEM
While not as cold-hardy as pansies, many petunias tolerate light frosts and continue blooming well into autumn, extending their season and providing color when summer annuals fade.

WHAT TO KNOW
Their prolific flowering makes them perfect for beds and containers. And, as a bonus, petunias are generally low-maintenance.

FAVORITE VARIETIES
Supertunia Vista Bubblegum, Capella Hello Yellow, Madness Series

FOR THE LOVE OF...

Fall Ferns

With their lush fronds, graceful arches, and verdant green color, it's no wonder that exuberant ferns are a staple in Southern gardens and in the hanging baskets and containers that grace front porches throughout the region. Generally speaking, autumn is an ideal time to plant ferns (try the Southern Shield or Autumn varieties) because the plants have a chance to establish their roots before spring and summer.

From the Kitchen

"It looked like the world was covered in a cobbler crust of brown sugar and cinnamon."
—Author and North Carolina native Sarah Addison Allen

The Southern Checklist
Fry Up Apple Fritters

·····◇·····

Bake Pumpkin Spice Monkey Bread

·····◇·····

Georgia pecans preferred.

Make Pecan-Crusted Chicken

·····◇·····

Perfect Your Skillet Cornbread

·····◇·····

Save Room for Sweet Potato Pie

And don't forget the marshmallows!

Batter Up

Apple Fritters

Take everything you love about apple cider doughnuts, and then fry it.

MAKES *6 servings*   **WORKING TIME** *25 minutes*   **TOTAL TIME** *30 minutes*

Canola oil, for frying

½ **cup granulated sugar**

1 **teaspoon apple pie spice, divided**

1¼ **cups all-purpose flour, spooned and leveled**

2 **tablespoons packed light brown sugar**

1½ **teaspoons baking powder**

¼ **teaspoon kosher salt**

½ **cup fresh apple cider**

1 **large egg**

1 **teaspoon pure vanilla extract**

1 **large Granny Smith apple**

1. Fill a large Dutch oven with 1½ inches oil and heat to 350°F (use a deep-fry thermometer to test the temperature). Set a cooling rack on a rimmed baking sheet. Combine granulated sugar and ½ teaspoon pie spice in a bowl; set aside.

2. Whisk together flour, brown sugar, baking powder, salt, and remaining ½ teaspoon pie spice in a bowl. Whisk together cider, egg, and vanilla in a separate bowl. Add wet ingredients to dry ingredients, and stir until just combined.

3. Peel and core apple. Coarsely grate half the apple and cut the other half into ¼-inch pieces. Gently fold into batter.

4. Working in batches, drop spoonfuls of the batter (about 2 tablespoons each) into oil. Fry, turning once, until golden brown, 2 to 4 minutes.

5. Toss warm fritters in sugar-spice mixture. Transfer to the cooling rack. Serve warm or at room temperature.

Rise and Shine

Pumpkin Spice Monkey Bread

—————◇—————

Inspired by RT Lodge in Maryville, Tennessee, this autumnal twist on a classic crowd-pleaser is just the thing to lure sleepyheads out of bed.

WORKING TIME *1 hour*   **TOTAL TIME** *2 hours 10 minutes*   **MAKES** *12 servings*

2¾ teaspoons instant yeast

2 tablespoons canola oil, plus more for bowl

2 tablespoons unsalted butter

1 cup, plus 2 tablespoons whole milk

1 large egg

3½ cups bread flour, spooned and leveled, plus more for work surface

½ cup sugar

⅓ teaspoon kosher salt

⅓ cup malted milk powder

Pumpkin Spice Glaze, Coffee Butter, and for serving, recipes following

1. Place yeast in a bowl. Lightly grease a separate bowl. Melt butter in a small saucepan over low heat. Add oil, milk, and egg. Cook, stirring frequently, until an instant-read thermometer reads 110°F. Pour over yeast and let sit until yeast is bubbling, 8 to 10 minutes.

2. Whisk together flour, sugar, salt, and malted milk powder in a bowl. Add dry ingredients to butter mixture. Beat with an electric mixer fit with a dough hook on low until ingredients come together. Increase speed to high and beat until the dough is glossy and elastic and pulls away from the sides of the bowl, 9 to 11 minutes. Transfer to prepared bowl and cover with plastic wrap. Refrigerate, 1 hour. While dough is resting, make the Coffee Butter, Spiced Sugar, and Pumpkin Spice Glaze.

3. Invert dough onto a floured work surface. Roll to a ½-inch-thick 8- by 16-inch rectangle. (The shape does not have to be perfect.) Spread ½ cup of the Coffee Butter on the dough all the way to the edges. Sprinkle 1 cup of the Spiced Sugar evenly across the dough. Roll dough into a log, starting at one short end.

4. Use a knife to cut the log into ½-inch-thick slices; cut slices into ½-inch pieces. Divide half of the dough between 2 8-inch cast-iron skillets. Top with remaining Coffee Butter and Spiced Sugar, dividing evenly. Top with remaining dough pieces, dividing evenly. Cover with plastic wrap and let rest, at room temperature, until dough rises slightly, about 45 minutes.

5. Preheat oven to 350°F. Place skillets on a rimmed baking sheet and bake until golden brown, 25 to 30 minutes. Drizzle with Pumpkin Spice Glaze. Serve warm.

Pumpkin Spice Glaze

Beat ¼ cup **heavy cream**, 3 tablespoons **pure pumpkin puree**, 1½ tablespoons **brewed coffee**, ¾ teaspoon **finely ground coffee**, ¾ teaspoon **pumpkin spice**, and ½ teaspoon **kosher salt** with an electric mixer on medium speed until smooth, 3 to 5 minutes. Reduce mixer speed to low and slowly beat in 1½ cups **confectioners' sugar** until smooth. *Makes 1 cup.*

Top it Off

Coffee Butter

Beat ⅔ cup room temperature **unsalted butter**, 1 tablespoon **finely ground coffee**, and ½ teaspoon **kosher salt** with an electric mixer on medium speed until combined and smooth, 1 to 2 minutes. *Makes ¾ cup.*

Spiced Sugar

Combine ¾ cup **granulated sugar**, ¾ cup packed **dark brown sugar**, 1½ teaspoons **finely ground coffee**, and 1 tablespoon **pumpkin spice** in a bowl. *Makes 2 cups.*

Try a Twist on a Classic

Pecan-Crusted Chicken with Honey-Mustard Sauce

With its satisfying panko and pecan coating, this oven-baked dish is ideal for both weeknight suppers and special occasions.

WORKING TIME *20 minutes* **TOTAL TIME** *50 minutes* **MAKES** *4 to 6 servings*

4 whole chicken legs, skins removed

Kosher salt and freshly ground black pepper

½ cup all-purpose flour

2 teaspoons finely chopped fresh rosemary

1 teaspoon smoked paprika

½ teaspoon ground cayenne

2 large eggs, well beaten

¾ cup finely chopped pecans

½ cup panko breadcrumbs

¼ cup Dijon mustard

¼ cup mayonnaise

¼ cup pure honey

2 tablespoons apple cider vinegar

1. Preheat oven to 425°F. Season chicken with salt and pepper. Whisk together flour, rosemary, paprika, and cayenne in a shallow bowl. Season with salt and pepper. Place eggs in a second shallow bowl. Season with salt and pepper. Combine pecans and panko in a third shallow bowl. Season with salt and pepper.

2. Working with one piece at a time, dredge chicken in flour mixture, turning to coat, then in egg (allowing excess to drip off), then in pecan mixture, pressing to help adhere; place on a rimmed baking sheet. Repeat with remaining chicken, flour, eggs, and pecan mixtures. Bake until the internal temperature on an instant-read thermometer reads 165°F, 30 to 35 minutes.

3. Meanwhile combine mustard, mayonnaise, honey, and vinegar in a bowl. Serve alongside chicken.

PRIDE OF PLACE

The Pecan Capital of the World

Providing roughly 80 percent of the planet's production, the United States is the leading global supplier of pecans, the only major tree nut indigenous to America. Georgia claims the country's bragging rights, with an average pecan harvest exceeding 100 million pounds (that's a whole lot of pecan pies). Most production, which happens during the peak season of October through November, is centered in Albany and Dougherty County, a region dubbed the Pecan Capital of the World. Of Algonquian origin, the word *pecan* (used to describe all nuts requiring a stone to crack) dates to 1712, when it sounded like "puh-con," but in modern use the correct pronunciation is however your grandma said it.

Pull Out the Cast-Iron

Skillet Cornbread

———◇———

Mississippi Native Erin Napier (of HGTV's *Home Town*) knows a thing or two about community, and her rich and buttery recipe will be the talk of the town.

WORKING TIME *15 minutes*   **TOTAL TIME** *40 minutes*   **MAKES** *10 servings*

6 **tablespoons unsalted butter, divided, plus more for serving**

1 **cup all-purpose flour, spooned and leveled**

1 **cup self-rising white cornmeal mix, spooned and leveled**

2 **tablespoons sugar**

2⅓ **cups buttermilk**

2 **large eggs**

½ **teaspoon freshly ground black pepper.**

1. Preheat oven to 450°F. Heat 2 tablespoons butter in a 10-inch cast-iron skillet in oven, 5 minutes.

2. Whisk together flour, cornmeal mix, and sugar in a bowl. Melt remaining 4 tablespoons butter. Whisk together buttermilk, eggs, and melted butter in a separate bowl. Add wet ingredients to dry ingredients and stir to combine. Carefully pour batter in hot pan. Sprinkle with pepper.

3. Bake until golden brown, 20 to 25 minutes. Serve warm topped with butter.

Know-How

MAKE YOUR OWN BUTTER

All you need is an ordinary electric stand mixer and a little cheesecloth to whip up your own spread. First, layer a strainer with three layers of cheesecloth and set over a bowl. Whisk **2 cups heavy whipping cream** on high speed with an electric stand mixer until pale yellow and liquid separates from solids, 8 to 10 minutes. Transfer to the lined strainer. Gather cheesecloth around the solids and knead, forming a ball and squeezing out excess liquid. Rinse well under cold water. Remove from cheesecloth and pat dry with paper towels. Season with **fine sea salt**, if desired, or one of the below combos. Shape into a log. Use immediately or chill, wrapped in plastic, up to 2 weeks.

SWEET HOT

• 2 tablespoons red pepper jelly

• 2 tablespoons Sriracha

• ¾ teaspoon freshly ground black pepper

CITRUS SERRANO

• 1 tablespoon lime zest

• 1 tablespoon lemon zest

• 1 tablespoon orange zest

• 1 large minced garlic clove

• 1 minced Serrano pepper

• Freshly ground black pepper

BOURBON MAPLE NUT

• ⅓ cup finely chopped roasted salted almonds

• 2 tablespoons maple syrup

• 1½ tablespoons bourbon

Save Room For...

Sweet Potato Pie

———— ◇ ————

Sweet potatoes thrive in Tar Heel territory, where almost 100,000 acres
of the official North Carolina vegetable are harvested each year. A toasted marshmallow
pie topping is a sweet salute to the confection's casserole counterpart.

WORKING TIME *25 minutes* **TOTAL TIME** *6 hours 10 minutes (includes cooling)* **MAKES** *8 servings*

FOR THE CRUST

- 1½ **cups graham cracker crumbs**
- 3 **tablespoons granulated sugar**
- ½ **teaspoon kosher salt**
- ½ **cup (1 stick) unsalted butter, melted**

FOR THE FILLING

- 2 **medium (about 12 ounces each) sweet potatoes**
- 3 **large eggs, at room temperature**
- ⅔ **cup packed light brown sugar**
- ⅓ **cup granulated sugar**
- ½ **cup half-and-half**
- 4 **tablespoons (½ stick) unsalted butter, melted**
- 1 **teaspoon pure vanilla extract**
- ½ **teaspoon kosher salt**
- ½ **teaspoon ground cinnamon**
- ½ **teaspoon ground ginger**
- ¼ **teaspoon freshly grated nutmeg**

Pinch ground cloves

- ½ **cup mini marshmallows**
- ½ **cup regular marshmallows, halved crosswise**

1. Make the crust: Preheat oven to 350°F. Stir together graham cracker crumbs, sugar, and salt in a bowl. Add butter and stir with a fork until well-combined. Press into bottom and up the sides of a broiler-proof 9-inch pie plate. Bake until edges are just barely golden, 6 to 8 minutes. Cool on a wire rack.

2. Increase oven temperature to 400°F. Pierce potatoes several times with a fork. Bake on a rimmed baking sheet until tender in the center when pierced with a knife, 1 hour to 1 hour 20 minutes. Carefully slice potatoes in half lengthwise and let stand until cool enough to handle.

3. Reduce oven temperature to 375°F. Scoop potato flesh from skins into a food processor; discard skins. Process until smooth, about 1 minute. Measure out 1½ cups puree (save remaining puree for another use).

4. Whisk together eggs, brown sugar, and granulated sugar in a bowl. Whisk in half-and-half, butter, and vanilla. Whisk in potato puree, salt, cinnamon, ginger, nutmeg, and cloves. Pour into piecrust. Bake until filling is set around edges (will still jiggle slightly in center), 35 to 40 minutes. Let cool completely on a wire rack, about 3 hours. Pie may be chilled at this point, if desired.

5. Before serving, preheat oven to broil with oven rack 5 inches from the heat source. Wrap piecrust tightly with aluminum foil. Scatter marshmallows over top of pie, and broil until golden brown, rotating pie halfway through for even browning, 1 to 1½ minutes.

On the Go

"Autumn leaves don't fall, they fly. They take their time and wander on this their only chance to soar."
—**Author and Georgia native Delia Owens,** *Where the Crawdads Sing*

The Southern Checklist

Explore Highlands & Cashiers, North Carolina

⋯⋯◇⋯⋯

Balloon darts, meet your match.

Visit a State or County Fair

⋯⋯◇⋯⋯

Go Antiquing for Pie Collectibles

◆ **PLUS** ◆

More Southern Wit & Wisdom

Achieve potluck perfection!

INDULGE YOUR YONDERLUST

Highlands & Cashiers, North Carolina

L ike Johnny and June, these Blue Ridge Mountain towns are rarely mentioned without each other, although they hit different notes that combine to achieve high-altitude harmony. In Highlands, which fittingly sits at a higher elevation, visitors will discover a charming Main Street and a vibrant arts community nurtured by local institutions like the Bascom Center for Visual Arts. Just 10 miles to the east, the smaller Cashiers (pronounced Cash-ers) is home to the storied 1,400-acre High Hampton Resort, which has been charming guests for nearly a century. Wherever you choose to stay on the plateau, you'll be well positioned to enjoy stunning mountain views, winding hiking trails, and misty, majestic waterfalls.

CAROLINA 'CUE EXPLAINED

Visitors to Western North Carolina should seek out the region's signature Lexington-style (also known as Piedmont-style) barbecue. It features a subtly sweet vinegar sauce with a hint of tomato, not to be confused with the more vinegary and peppery sauce of the Eastern style. Sauce aside, Carolinians across the state tend to share a preference for pork, which stems from the fact that the dense Carolina forests weren't particularly cattle-friendly.

Highlands & Cashiers

No. 1
Fly-Fishing Excursions
A trip here is not complete without catching (then releasing!) a rainbow trout. Brookings Anglers will be happy to guide you on your journey.

No. 2
Cozy Inns
From storied standouts like the High Hampton Resort and Old Edwards Inn (shown) to newer spots like Skyline Lodge, there's no shortage of high style in the hamlet.

No. 3
Antiquing Appeal
This neck of the woods is rich with storied finds, which you can shop for at spots such as Mantiques and Reclamations, or see on display at the collected Highlander Mountain House (here and far left).

No. 4
Scenic Hikes
The 2.2-mile hike along Whiteside Mountain in Cashiers offers seriously gorgeous fall foliage in mid-October.

More Small Towns to Explore in Fall

MENTONE, ALABAMA
Nestled atop Lookout Mountain, this quaint village in Northeast Alabama is a draw for outdoors enthusiasts, as is nearby DeSoto State Park.

HERMANN, MISSOURI
The jewel of the Missouri Rhineland *willkommens* fall visitors with wineries, wurst hauses, and dozens of other delightful ways to enjoy its German heritage.

BEREA, KENTUCKY
Creatives, take note. This town is the beating heart of the folk Arts and Crafts scenes in the state. Pop by the historic Boone Tavern Hotel while you're there.

Visit a State or County Fair

Step right up! Although the region hosts its fair share of Ferris-wheeled events during the summer (Mississippi's famed Neshoba County Fair comes to mind), the funnel cakes *really* get frying come September and into October, when everything from small-town celebrations to the behemoth known as the Texas State Fair boot up.

There's something about the year-after-year consistency of these traditions—the familiar foods on a stick, the same old satin beauty queen sashes, that one adrenaline rush of a ride everyone always talks about (lookin' at you, Zipper!)—that deliver as much joy and comfort as a lovably tacky plush toy. (*Psst*: See right for how to win one.)

Essential Fair Rites of Passage

No. 1
Animal Interactions
Whether it's rooster crowing contests or livestock showings in the 4-H barn, friendly faces—feathered or furry—are part of the draw.

No. 2
Fair Games
You haven't truly fair-ed unless you've played balloon darts. Tip: To pop 'em, experts say to throw (hard!) in a high arc motion to approach from above.

No. 3
Arts & Crafts
From colorful potholders to pieced quilts to photography, it's a joy to take in the talents of creatives from the community.

No. 4
Prize Produce
Because you simply haven't lived until you've laid eyes on a 1,100 pound pumpkin.

A SHORT (AND SWEET) HISTORY OF...

Cotton Candy

You can thank, of all people, a Tennessee dentist for this machine-spun confection. In 1897, Nashville doc William Morrison teamed up with candymaker pal John C. Wharton to create this air-spun sweet known as "fairy floss." They sold a whopping 68,000 boxes of it for a quarter each at the 1904 World's Fair in St. Louis. Later in 1921, when Morrison's patent expired, Josef Lascaux of Louisiana—also a dentist!—reinvented a similar machine to make what he called cotton candy. That name proved as sticky as the treat itself.

Go Antiquing for Pie Collectibles

Preparing and presenting dessert with timeworn wares* means your recipes are seasoned with generations of sweet memories.

Assuming they're still food-safe, of course

No. 1
TIN PIE PLATES

Throughout the 1950s, pie companies sold their creations in metal pie tins, which were meant to be returned after the pie was consumed. The graphic embossed logos served as important advertising tools.

No. 2
PIE BIRDS

Inspired by an old nursery rhyme, the ceramic vessel's vented structure allows steam to escape during baking, thus preventing filling overflow disasters.

No. 3
ROLLING PINS

Made from wood, porcelain, marble, and handblown glass, these cylindrical staples are also pretty clustered in a crock when not in use.

No. 4
PASTRY CRIMPERS

Also known as "jaggers," these were popularized in the 19th century, as pies both savory and sweet became common at mealtimes across Europe.

No. 5
PIE SERVERS

These triangular servers are easily scouted at flea markets and estate sales. Look for variety in handle material, as Bakelite, wood, and porcelain were all common.

FALL WIT & WISDOM

More ways to embrace the season in its autumnal best.

Perfect the Potluck

·····◇·····

Divide and Conquer

To avoid over-indexing on broccoli salad, designate categories based on the first letter of the attendees' last names (A–G: mains; H–L: salads and sides, etc.). To accommodate everyone, consider designations such as "nondairy" or "gluten-free."

Address Other Needs

Utensils like serving spoons and spatulas often go overlooked, as do trash bags. Plan accordingly.

Label Your Dish

If you want to be reunited with your precious Pyrex, be sure to stake your claim. Jotting your name on the bottom with nail polish means it won't wash off in the dishwasher.

DESIGN WITH A DRAWL

Decorating with Books

A home with books that spill into every nook and out of every cranny conveys a limitless curiosity. Plus, it provides a friendly, get-to-know-ya glimpse at whatever makes the homeowner's spirit sing, be it historical fiction, offbeat humor, or the short stories of Flannery O'Connor. Stock up on titles from the South's best indie bookstores—try Square Books in Oxford, Mississippi, Parnassus Books in Nashville, Tennessee, or Sundog Books in Seaside, Florida—then display your books on a coffee table or bundle titles with twine on a console.

NOW PLAYING

Compile a Playlist

Mississippi native Erin Napier (HGTV's *Home Town*) shares what's on repeat this time of year at her store, Laurel Mercantile.

·····◇·····

"How to Dream"
by Sam Phillips

"More of You"
by Chris Stapleton

"Time Honored Tradition"
by Natalie Hemby

"Cover Me Up"
by Jason Isbell

"A Wink and a Smile "
by Harry Connick Jr.

"A Sorta Fairytale"
by Tori Amos

"Somewhere Only We Know"
by Keane

"A Dream of Home"
by Tyler Ramsey

IDENTIFICATION KEY

Fall Foliage

Leaf peepers, take note: These are some of the more showy specimens you're likely to encounter on a seasonal stroll.

Sassafras

Japanese Maple

Black Tupelo

ONLY IN THE SOUTH...

QUIRKY GAME-DAY TRADITIONS

There's no shortage of kooky collegiate customs. To name a few: Auburn University students celebrate wins by slinging rolls of toilet paper over oak tree branches outside Toomer's Drugstore. Mississippi State fans ring cowbells for good luck. University of Tennessee devotees can be found "sailgating" in boats along the Tennessee River, while Texas A&M students look to "Yell Leaders" to practice midnight cheers before big games.

HOME REMEDY

Shine Up Copper

Unless you're firmly in the "let it patina" camp, you can clean up tarnished copper with ketchup. Simply spread a few tablespoons on the surface of the pot, then use a soft brush or gloved fingers to rub it in using gentle pressure. (Don't be alarmed: The mixture will darken as it breaks down the dirt.) Rinse with water, and buff with a dry cotton cloth.

AROUND THE SOUTH

FALL HAPPENINGS

Gather round for music and makers.

John C. Campbell Folk School Festival
Brasstown, North Carolina

Shop more than 200 vendors, enjoy live demos (fiber arts, woodworking, blacksmithing...), and enjoy bluegrass at this ode to Appalachia.

National Storytelling Festival
Jonesborough, Tennessee

World-renowned storytellers convene in the state's oldest town to share tales with 10,000-plus enthusiastic listeners.

Ocmulgee Indigenous Celebration
Macon, Georgia

Hosted by the National Park Service and the Ocmulgee Mounds Association in coordination with the Muscogee (Creek) Nations, this annual event features traditional dancing, music, and art.

Kentuck Festival of the Arts
Northport, Alabama

Going strong for more than 50 years, this juried arts festival includes more than 260 vendors and features folk and contemporary crafts.

Red Maple   **Aspen**   **Sugar Maple**

LODGING OFF
Designed by Richard
Keith Langham, this
Mississippi Delta hunting
lodge remains happily
disconnected (read: spotty
Wi-Fi), which means more
time spent by the Tennessee
limestone fireplace.

Birds of Mississippi
MISSISSIPPIANS
THE HUNTING BOOK

Holidays

It's Not the *Holidays* in the South Without...

·····◇·····

Siblings or cousins in matching pajamas on Christmas Eve

◇

The assembly line of food gift prep for the neighbors, teachers, the mail carrier, your third cousin twice removed...

◇

Stocking the bar with bourbon and enough cheese straws to fuel a small-town parade

◇

The unbridled joy (and buying of milk) that comes with any dusting of snow

◇

Pulling out your favorite punch bowl in anticipation of mixing up a big-batch beverage

◇

Festooning every room with lush greenery (also: Using the word *festooning*)

◇

The satisfaction that comes with a pristinely wrapped gift—after all, Southerners love to put bows on things

Around the House

"No matter what, I always make it home for Christmas."
—Country icon and Tennessee native Dolly Parton

The Southern Checklist

And a cute
card display
to boot!

Create a Festive Porch

⋯⋯◇⋯⋯

Cook Up a Warm Glow

⋯⋯◇⋯⋯

Polish Your Silver

Poinsettias or
paperwhites?

⋯⋯◇⋯⋯

Embrace Blooms & Berries

⋯⋯◇⋯⋯

Hang a Southern Stocking

⋯⋯◇⋯⋯

Design a Warm Welcome

Create a Festive Porch

Southerners love a good twirl up, and this time of year, that appreciation of pomp and circumstance is as strong as your craziest aunt's hot toddy. The trick: Make sure the size of your swag fits the scale of your home. Southerners, including author and designer James Farmer, don't do dinky. Here, his home in Perry, Georgia—known as Farmdale Cottage—gets gussied up with all-natural arrangements. "Colonial Williamsburg is the ultimate inspiration," says James, who also says he takes decorative cues from Southern coastal towns, including Charleston and New Orleans.

NO. 1
Sunny Citrus

Touches of produce lend pops of color to a swag of cypress. "I call it grocery store decor," says James. "Simple oranges and lemons from Publix can be so beautiful."

NO. 2
Pineapple Focal Point

Sea captains often displayed the exotic fruit on their gates to signify their return home from voyages, and it has since become a Southern symbol of hospitality.

NO. 3
Magnolia Garland

"Magnolia is the backbone of Southern holiday decor," says James. "The velvety brown backs and shiny green leaves look so beautiful with red berries and citrus."

NO. 4
Satin Ribbon

"While red velvet and evergreen are always in style, I like to bring an interior aesthetic to the outside with lighter greens, coral, peach, and cream satin," says James.

GRILLED ORANGE OLD-FASHIONED

If you're decorating with citrus, consider this a fittingly thematic way to toast your work. Heat a grill to medium-high. Grill slices of one **navel orange,** turning slightly occasionally, just until charred, 2 to 4 minutes. Muddle oranges, 4 dashes **Angostura bitters,** and 4 **Maraschino cherries** in a pitcher until fruit is mashed. Stir in 8 ounces of **bourbon** or **rye**. *Makes 4 servings.*

Cook Up a Warm Glow

———————— ◆ ————————

Yet another reason to spring for the next dough bowl you run across
at the antiques store: It makes for a beautiful menorah. Fill the
wooden bowl with floral foam, insert candles (we love the simplicity of
plain old white), and nestle seasonal greenery between the tapers.

OY TO THE WORLD
*Founded in 1749,
the Kahal Kadosh Beth
Elohim in Charleston,
South Carolina, is the
oldest continuously operating
synagogue—and the
second-oldest synagogue
building—in the
United States.*

DISPLAY SEASON'S GREETINGS

No. 1
BASKET BEVY
Show off merry mailings on a vintage tobacco basket by tucking cards into the overlapping strips of reed.

No. 2
FIR KEEPS
Let your family tree overflow with good tidings by securing cards to jute rope with mini-clothespins.

No. 3
BRANCHING OUT
Clip or string cards onto a magnolia garland, then drape it across a mantel, around a door frame, or over a hutch.

No. 4
SLEIGH ALL DAY
When propped up against a wall, an old sled is a clever spot to showcase a wintry mix of well wishes.

TAKE A SHINE
While you'll encounter many a home remedy to maintain silver's sparkle, in-the-know Southerners swear by 150-year-old Wright's Silver Cream.

Polish Your Silver

W hile we're ardent proponents of using the "good stuff" year-round, there's no time like the holiday season to pull out your most precious silver and silver plate heirlooms. (Tip: Pure silver is not magnetic, so if a magnet sticks to your piece, it's likely silver plated.)

Antique ice buckets, in particular, infuse an event with celebratory spirit. The collectibles hearken back to the days before commercial ice makers, when ice was costly to consume. As such, Southerners able to afford the extravagance to chill wine and Champagne conspicuously displayed their precious cubes.

EMBRACE BLOOMS & BERRIES

No. 1
POINSETTIA
Tucked into glass jars, poinsettia clippings bring a burst of color to the mantel. (The plant is named after South Carolinian Joel R. Poinsett, the first U.S. ambassador to Mexico.)

No. 2
PAPERWHITES
These perennials are easy to grow inside—they need only a potting element (marbles, pebbles), water, and a 3- to 4-inch-deep vessel.

No. 3
HOLLY BRANCHES
Stuffed with clippings from a backyard holly bush, an antique wicker grape harvest basket has dramatic impact in a historic house's foyer.

No. 4
AMARYLLIS
To craft a festive display, arrange bulbs in an assortment of vintage brass vessels—each should be roughly one inch wider than its bulb—with well-draining potting mix.

HANG A SOUTHERN STOCKING

No. 1
FARM CHARM
Personalized with custom chain-stitch lettering, humble feed bags enjoy new life in stocking form.

No. 2
COASTAL COZY
Cable-knit stockings feel at home in a salty-air setting, especially with a life preserver "wreath" and anchor andirons.

No. 3
SACK PACK
Traditionally used to haul grain to the mills, grain sack fabric featured stripes or patterns to distinguish the farmer.

No. 4
PLAID TIDINGS
Upcycled tartan fringed wool blankets in varying color combinations make for a very merry mantel.

Design a Warm Welcome

The Bedecked Doorways of Colonial Williamsburg

If you've been lucky enough to visit Virginia's living history museum during the holiday season, then you know the 300-acre property is chock-full of inspiration for decking out your doorway, a tradition that started in 1936. To bring it all to life, Joanna Chapman, the landscape director of the Colonial Williamsburg Foundation, says the decorating process, which begins right after Thanksgiving, takes a full two weeks and focuses on all-natural materials—Fraser fir, white pine—that would have been familiar to the colonists. (Case in point: Poinsettias, which weren't introduced in the U.S. until 1825, aren't allowed.) Joanne adds that one of the most notable elements of what has come to be known as the "Williamsburg" style is the use of fresh fruit on the Historic Area buildings, including the Apple Fans hung above doors and the Della Robbia–style wreaths.

As soon as those leafy fall garlands lose their luster, it's time to shift into holiday mode. Mind you, this is no time for minimalism: Here, the more is the merrier, as demonstrated by this Little Rock entry by Arkansas designer Christina Gore. "My client had a giant magnolia tree in her backyard, so we incorporated larger branches that give the garland more of a wild and organic look," she says. Giant gold-edged red bows—for exteriors, Christina recommends ribbon that's at least four inches thick—and pine cones serve up traditional touches, while giant jingle bells bring the whimsy. "I love the natural, but I also love adding a touch of magic to it."

At the Table

◇

"Cooking done with care is an act of love."
Author, food critic, and Mississippi native Craig Claiborne

*Start clipping
those camellias.*

The Southern Checklist
Set a Southern Christmas Table

·····◇·····

Pick Your Place Setting

·····◇·····

Arrange a Seasonal Centerpiece

·····◇·····

Host a Wreath-Making Party

*Hot toddies for
everyone!*

Set a Southern Christmas Table

Y ou can thank a group of determined citizens from Alabama's Butler County for the camellia's designation as the state's official flower in 1959. Until then, the goldenrod claimed the proverbial podium, but a sneeze-inducing weed simply couldn't compete with the elegant camellia, one of few plants that bloom during their dormancy. "I love how they stand out against all the greenery and pine this time of year," says Birmingham, Alabama–based stylist Kathleen Varner, who prettied up the holiday table shown here.

NO. 1
Cranberry Transferware

The vintage dishes are a muted-yet-merry twist on the typically more vibrant reds of the season and pair well with a nubby brown linen tablecloth.

NO. 2
Crystal Coupes

The rose-colored glassware feels "fancy and special," says Kathleen. "That's what we're all striving for this time of year."

NO. 3
Camellia Clippings

Strewn down the table runner-style (and on plates), the bold blooms make for a festive and fragrant focal point.

NO. 4
Shiny-Brite Ornaments

The hand-blown glass baubles from the 1940s and '50s "add just the right amount of shine," says Kathleen, who insists that every table needs something old.

PICK YOUR PLACE SETTING

No. 1
SOUTHERN BELL
Slide handwritten name
cards into the slots
of sleigh bells, and give
new meaning to
"be there with bells on."

No. 2
MINTY FRESH
Pair red ticking stripe
table linens with
clippings of rosemary
secured to a wire in
a candy cane shape.

No. 3
TREE TOPPER
Virginian Jenny Bohannon
combined classic
cabbageware with a
sweet napkin "tree" and
dove ornament.

No. 4
WESTERN WHIMSY
Savannah bakery
owner Cheryl Day
gives bandanas a
festive touch by tying
them with tinsel.

Arrange a Seasonal Centerpiece

Create candy canelike stripes by placing a small pillar vessel inside a larger vase and filling the gaps between the two with red and white marbles. Contrast the colorful stack with anemones, garden roses, and evergreen sprigs.

Host a Wreath-Making Party

Invite a few friends over for hot toddies and this hands-on approach to holiday entertaining, which starts with materials foraged from your own backyard.

HOTTY TODDY!
Anyone who has ever attended a tailgate at the University of Mississippi has likely heard this fan-favorite phrase on repeat. Some say it takes its inspiration from the whiskey-based cocktail (shown at left), although others insist it derives from a chant used during WWII.

Cinnamon Hot Toddy with Cinnamon-Sugar Rim

WORKING TIME *20 minutes*
TOTAL TIME *20 minutes*
MAKES *6 servings (about 3½ cups)*

- ½ cup pure honey
- 6 (3-inch) strips lemon rind, plus ½ cup lemon juice, reserving rinds
- 2 cinnamon sticks, broken in half, plus more for garnish
- 2 cups bourbon
- 2 tablespoons sugar
- ¼ teaspoon ground cinnamon
- Lemon and orange slices, for garnish

1. Combine honey, lemon rind and juice, cinnamon sticks, and ¾ cup water in a medium saucepan. Cook over medium-low heat, stirring frequently, until mixture is steaming, 4 to 6 minutes. Stir in bourbon.

2. Combine sugar and ground cinnamon in small dish. Rub rims of 6 mugs with reserved lemon rind and dip in cinnamon sugar mixture, pressing to coat. Serve toddy, warm, in sugar-rimmed mugs garnished with cinnamon stick, and lemon and orange slices.

Caramelized Onion, Bacon, and Gruyère Fondue

WORKING TIME *45 minutes*
TOTAL TIME *45 minutes*
MAKES *6 to 8 servings*

- 1½ pounds Gruyère, grated
- 1½ tablespoons cornstarch
- 4 slices bacon, chopped
- 1 medium sweet onion, sliced
- 1 tablespoon butter
- 1 cup dry white wine
- Kosher salt and freshly ground black pepper
- Freshly ground nutmeg, to taste
- Pretzel bites and sliced salami, for dipping

1. Toss together Gruyère and cornstarch in a bowl until coated. Cook bacon in a large Dutch oven over medium heat, stirring frequently, until crisp, 8 to 10 minutes. Transfer bacon to a bowl with a slotted spoon. Add onion and butter to Dutch oven. Cook over medium-low heat, stirring frequently, until onion is golden brown, 18 to 20 minutes. Transfer to bowl with bacon.

2. Increase heat to medium. Add wine to Dutch oven and cook until simmering. Reduce heat to low. Whisk in cheese by the handful, until melted. Stir in reserved bacon and onion. Season with salt, pepper, and nutmeg. Serve immediately with pretzel bites and sliced salami for dipping.

Almond-and-Chocolate Toffee

This sweet and buttery confection is one of the region's favorite food gifts.

WORKING TIME *35 minutes* **TOTAL TIME** *2 hours 35 minutes* **MAKES** *2½ pounds*

Cooking spray
- 2 **cups (4 sticks) unsalted butter**
- 2⅔ **cups sugar**
- 2 **tablespoons light Karo syrup**
- ⅔ **cup roasted almonds, chopped, plus more for topping**
- 1 **teaspoon pure vanilla extract**
- 1 **cup (6 ounces) milk chocolate chips**

1. Lightly grease a large rimmed baking sheet. Melt butter in a medium saucepan, with a candy thermometer attached, over medium heat. Add sugar and stir until dissolved, 8 to 10 minutes. Add karo syrup and 6 tablespoons water and stir to combine. Cook, stirring constantly, until mixture reaches 200°F. Add nuts and cook, stirring constantly, until mixture reaches 285°F. Remove from heat and stir in vanilla. Transfer mixture to prepared pan.

2. Sprinkle chocolate chips evenly over surface and let stand 5 minutes. Spread chocolate with an offset spatula and top with additional almonds. Let cool completely. Break into pieces and store in refrigerator in an airtight container.

A SHORT HISTORY OF....

Southern-Made Sweets

While nothing beats a homemade food gift, these regional delicacies are sure to please in a pinch.

Goo Goo Cluster
Nashville's Standard Candy Company invented America's first combination candy bar in 1912. It features milk chocolate, caramel, peanuts, and marshmallow nougat.

MoonPie
In 1917, a Kentucky coal miner asked snack salesman Earl Mitchell for a snack "as big as the moon." Earl reported back and the bakery obliged with the MoonPie. Now the Chattanooga-based company makes 1 million a day.

Little Debbie
Founder O.D. McKee got his start in the sweets biz in the 1930s, but it wasn't until 1960 that the brand came to be in Collegedale, Tennessee. O.D.'s granddaughter Debbie inspired the name and sits on the board.

· HOLIDAYS ·

From the Kitchen

◇

"You don't need a silver fork to eat good food."
—Chef and Louisiana native Paul Prudhomme

The Southern Checklist
Pour Brandy Milk Punch

·····◇·····

With cream cheese frosting, of course!

Bake Gingerbread Cinnamon Rolls

·····◇·····

Serve Asiago Cheese Biscuits and Bacon-Wrapped Peppadews

·····◇·····

Make Pork Tenderloin with Cinnamon-Clove Clementine Glaze

·····◇·····

Enjoy Merry Cherry Hand Pies

Get in the Spirits

Brandy Milk Punch

———————◇———————

Not quite as thick as eggnog (see: no eggs, less dairy), this wintry warmer
is a beloved staple of Acadiana. (Psst: Purists insist you use Napoleon brandy.)

WORKING TIME *5 minutes*   **TOTAL TIME** *5 hours*   **MAKES** *4 servings*

½ **cup cognac**

½ **cup dark rum**

2 **cups whole milk**

4 **tablespoons
   confectioners' sugar**

**Freshly grated nutmeg,
   for garnish**

1. Combine cognac, rum, milk, and confectioners' sugar in a blender.

2. Blend on high until fully frothy, 20 to 30 seconds.

3. Transfer to four glasses or a punch bowl.

4. Serve over ice garnished with fresh nutmeg.

A SHORT HISTORY OF...

Punch

Punch likely originated with British expats in India—some claim that the name came
from *panch,* the Hindu word for "five," denoting the typical amount of ingredients.
While the big-batch beverage fell out of favor after advancements in ice production
made prepping single-serve cocktails significantly easier, Southerners held on to
the communal ritual as tightly as their finest silver. These days, favorites tend to vary by
region. While in New Orleans, you're more likely to encounter frothy milk punch;
in Charleston, South Carolina, it'll likely be rum- and pineapple-based Planter's Punch;
and, in Richmond, expect to encounter Quoit Club Punch, a potent blend that
includes rum, cognac, and Madeira. Word to the wise: Hunch punch (aka "frat party
punch") should be avoided at all costs.

Try a Twist on a Classic

Gingerbread Cinnamon Rolls

———◇———

These rolled treats nestle perfectly in a large square kraft box, which means
they also make for an easy, on-the-go hostess gift.

WORKING TIME *25 minutes*   **TOTAL TIME** *2 hours 55 minutes (includes resting)*   **MAKES** *12 servings*

FOR THE DOUGH

- 2 tablespoons unsalted butter, at room temperature, plus more for bowl
- ¼ cup granulated sugar
- 1 tablespoon dry active yeast (not instant or rapid rise)
- 1 teaspoon ground cinnamon
- ¾ teaspoon ground ginger
- ½ teaspoon kosher salt
- ⅛ teaspoon ground cloves
- 3½ cups all-purpose flour, divided, plus more for work surface
- 1 cup whole milk
- 1 large egg
- 2 tablespoons molasses

FOR THE FILLING AND ASSEMBLY

- ½ cup packed light brown sugar
- 6 tablespoons unsalted butter, at room temperature, plus more for pan
- 1 tablespoon ground cinnamon
- 1½ teaspoons ground ginger
- ¼ teaspoon ground cloves

FOR THE TOPPING

- 4 ounces cream cheese, at room temperature
- ½ teaspoon pure vanilla extract
- 1⅓ cups confectioners sugar, divided
- 2 teaspoons molasses
- 1 to 2 teaspoons warm water

1. Make the dough: Lightly butter a bowl. Whisk together sugar, yeast, cinnamon, ginger, salt, cloves, and 1¾ cups flour in a bowl. Combine milk and butter in a small saucepan. Cook over low heat until the butter has melted and mixture reads between 105°F and 110°F on an instant-read thermometer.

2. Add milk mixture, egg, and molasses to flour mixture. Beat with an electric mixer, with a dough hook attached, on low speed until moistened. Continue beating, gradually adding remaining 1¾ cups flour, until smooth and pliable, 4 to 5 minutes.

3. Transfer dough to prepared bowl; cover with plastic wrap or a dish towel. Set bowl in a warm place and let rise until doubled in size, about 1 hour.

4. Make the filling and assemble: Combine brown sugar, butter, cinnamon, ginger, and cloves in a bowl.

5. Butter a 9- by 13-inch or 8- by 8-inch baking dish. On a lightly floured surface, roll dough into a 12- by 16-inch rectangle. Top with cinnamon-sugar mixture. Starting from the long side, roll up into a log. Cut into 12 (if using a 9- by 13-inch baking dish) or 9 (if using an 8- by 8-inch baking dish) pieces and place, cut sides up, in prepared dish. Cover with a dish towel and let rise until doubled in size, about 1 hour. Preheat oven to 375°F. Bake until cooked through and lightly browned, 20 to 25 minutes.

6. Make the topping: Combine cream cheese, vanilla, and 1 cup confectioners' sugar in a bowl. Whisk together molasses, water, and remaining ⅓ cup confectioners sugar in a separate bowl. Spread cream cheese mixture on warm rolls, then drizzle with molasses glaze.

Keep 'em Appetized

Asiago Cheese Biscuits and Bacon-Wrapped Peppadews

As far as small bites go, there's not a more crowd-pleasing combo than mini-biscuit sandwiches and bacon-wrapped anything.

WORKING TIME *65 minutes* **TOTAL TIME** *40 minutes plus 1½ hours* **MAKES** *8 servings*

FOR THE BISCUITS

- 2½ cups all-purpose flour, spooned and leveled, plus more for work surface
- 1½ tablespoons baking powder
- 1 teaspoon kosher salt
- ½ teaspoon freshly ground black pepper
- ½ cup (1 stick) cold unsalted butter, cut into pieces, plus 1 tablespoon melted butter, divided, plus more for serving
- 3 ounces Asiago cheese, grated (about ¾ cup)
- 1 cup buttermilk

Flaky sea salt, for garnish

Thinly sliced prosciutto, for serving

FOR THE PEPPADEWS

- 1 (4-ounce) log goat cheese, at room temperature
- 2 ounces cream cheese, at room temperature
- ¼ teaspoon garlic powder
- ¼ teaspoon onion powder

Kosher salt and freshly ground black pepper

- 30 Peppadew peppers (about 1 quart), drained and patted dry
- 10 slices regular (not thick-cut) bacon, cut crosswise into thirds

1. Make the biscuits: Preheat oven to 400°F. Line a baking sheet with parchment paper. Whisk together flour, baking powder, salt, and pepper in a bowl. Cut in cold butter with a pastry blender or two forks until mixture resembles small pebbles. Add Asiago and toss to coat. Add buttermilk and stir just until dough comes together.

2. Transfer dough to a lightly floured work surface. Gather into a ball then pat to ¾ inch thick. Cut biscuits with a 2-inch round cutter. Reroll and cut scraps. Place on prepared baking sheet, arranging in the shape of a Christmas tree and allowing edges of biscuits to touch. Brush tops with melted butter and sprinkle with flaky sea salt.

3. Bake until golden brown, 14 to 16 minutes. Serve with butter and prosciutto alongside.

4. Make the peppadews: Preheat oven to 350°F. Fit a rimmed baking sheet with a wire rack. Stir together goat cheese, cream cheese, garlic powder, and onion powder in a bowl. Season with salt and pepper. Transfer to a zip-top bag, and cut a small hole in one corner. Fill peppers with cheese mixture. Wrap each with bacon, securing with a toothpick. Place on prepared rack, filling side up. Freeze 20 minutes.

5. Bake until bacon is cooked through, 25 to 35 minutes. Let cool slightly before serving.

Serve a Festive Supper

Pork Tenderloin with Cinnamon-Clove Clementine Glaze

———— ◇ ————

Whole clementines—peels and all—can be blended up to make a decadent glaze for a dinner party–worthy main dish.

WORKING TIME *15 minutes*   **TOTAL TIME** *24 hours 40 minutes (includes chilling)*   **MAKES** *8 servings*

- 1 **clementine, skin on, quartered, plus more, sliced, for garnish**
- ¾ **cup packed light brown sugar**
- 1 **tablespoon white wine vinegar**
- 1 ½ **teaspoons fresh rosemary, plus more sprigs for garnish**
- 1 ½ **teaspoons country-style Dijon mustard**
- 1 **teaspoon ground cinnamon**
- ⅛ **teaspoon ground cloves**
- **Kosher salt and freshly ground black pepper**
- 2 **pork tenderloins (3 to 4 pounds total)**

1. Pulse together quartered clementine, sugar, vinegar, rosemary, mustard, cinnamon, and cloves in a food processor or blender until finely chopped. Chill 24 hours.

2. Preheat oven to 425°F. Line a rimmed baking sheet with aluminum foil. Place pork on prepared baking sheet and season with salt and pepper. Brush tenderloins on all sides with glaze. Roast until an instant-read thermometer inserted in the thickest part registers 145°F, 15 to 20 minutes. Let rest 5 minutes before slicing. Garnish with clementine slices and rosemary sprigs

Save Room for Dessert

Merry Cherry Hand Pies

———— ◇ ————

Adding cream cheese to the crust gives it a nice tangy flavor
and makes the dough soft, pliable, and easy to work. Feel free to substitute
other fruits, such as peach, blueberry, or strawberry, in the filling.

WORKING TIME *1 hour*   **TOTAL TIME** *4 hours (includes chilling)*   **MAKES** *12 hand pies*

FOR THE CRUST

- **3 cups all-purpose flour, spooned and leveled, plus more for work surface**
- **1 tablespoon granulated sugar**
- **1 teaspoon kosher salt**
- **1 cup (2 sticks) cold unsalted butter, cut into pieces**
- **4 ounces cold cream cheese, cut into pieces**

FOR THE FILLING

- **2½ tablespoons granulated sugar**
- **2 teaspoons cornstarch**
- **1¼ cups (6 ounces) frozen cherries**
- **1½ teaspoons fresh lemon juice**
- **⅛ teaspoon kosher salt**
- **⅛ teaspoon pure almond extract**
- **1 large egg, beaten**
- **1 tablespoon white sparkling sugar**

1. Make the crust: Pulse flour, sugar, and salt in a food processor until combined, 3 to 4 times. Add butter and cream cheese. Pulse until dough is pealike and shaggy, 14 to 16 times. Sprinkle 2 tablespoons water over dough, and process just until it begins to come together, 10 to 12 seconds. Transfer to a work surface, and shape into 2 discs (about 1 inch thick). Wrap discs in plastic wrap and refrigerate until firm, at least 1 hour and up to 2 days.

2. Make the filling: Whisk together granulated sugar and cornstarch in a small saucepan. Add cherries, lemon juice, and salt. Cook, stirring frequently, over medium heat, until mixture thickens and cherries begin to break down, 6 to 8 minutes. Remove from heat and stir in almond extract. Cool to room temperature. Chill until cold, at least 2 hours and up to 2 days.

3. Preheat oven to 375°F. Line two rimmed baking sheets with parchment paper. On a lightly floured work surface, roll one disc of dough to ⅛-inch thick. Use a 4-inch Christmas tree–shaped cookie cutter to cut out 12 trees. Transfer to prepared baking sheets. Spoon cherry mixture in center of each, dividing evenly (about 1 tablespoon each), leaving a ¼-inch border all around. Whisk together egg and 1 tablespoon water in a bowl. Brush borders with egg wash.

4. On a lightly floured work surface, roll remaining disc to ⅛ inch thick. Use cookie cutter to cut out 12 trees. Place on top of cherry filling–topped trees, and crimp edges with a fork. Brush tops with egg wash. Sprinkle with sparkling sugar, dividing evenly. Cut 3 slashes on top of each pie with a serrated knife. Refrigerate 30 minutes. Bake until golden brown, 15 to 18 minutes. Let cool 10 minutes before serving.

· HOLIDAYS ·

On the Go

"Life is either a daring adventure or nothing at all."
—Author, educator, advocate, and Alabama native Helen Keller

The Southern Checklist

Explore Middleburg, Virginia

Must love dogs.

·····◇·····

Visit a Carolina Tree Farm

·····◇·····

Go Antiquing for Quilts

◇ PLUS ◇

More Southern Wit & Wisdom

DIY a
Dolly Parton
tree topper!

INDULGE YOUR YONDERLUST

Middleburg, Virginia

Revelers seeking an old-fashioned Christmas need look no further than the heart of Virginia's horse and hunt country, where the small town of Middleburg (population 677) shines bright against a backdrop of the Blue Ridge Mountains. Although the town's just 50 miles from the nation's capital, you'll feel a world away once you line up along Washington Street for the Middleburg Christmas Parade and watch members of the Middleburg Hunt Club (above) trot through the town with dozens of loyal hounds alongside a steady procession of antique fire trucks and festive floats. Year-round visitors can slip on their waxed canvas jackets and mosey over to the six-acre National Sporting Library & Museum. Founded in 1954, it explores the heritage and history of foxhunting, steeplechasing, and other country hunt pastimes.

Middleburg

No. 1
Hearty Fare
Dining options span the spectrum, and the region's many cideries, wineries, and distilleries serve up plenty of beverages to wash it all down.

No. 2
Historic Inns and Time-Honored Taverns
Established in 1728, the charming Red Fox Inn & Tavern is thought to be America's oldest continuously operated inn. (George Washington even paid it a visit.)

No. 3
Cute Boutiques
Less than one mile long, the historic district is packed with shops of both the holiday and horse enthusiast variety.

No. 4
Merry Markets
Hosted in a 100-year-old farmhouse, the Lucketts Holiday House in nearby Leesburg is a must-visit for inspiring vignettes and contemporary and antique trimmings.

More Small Towns to Explore During the Holidays

DAHLONEGA, GEORGIA
Take in a show at the historic Holly Theatre before touring this chock-full-of-charm North Georgia town that has served as a Hallmark movie backdrop.

GRUENE, TEXAS
A two-steppin' Texas Christmas awaits (as does Cowboy Kringle!) in this once-bustling cotton-town-turned-thriving-historic-district.

BARDSTOWN, KENTUCKY
The Bourbon Capital of the World really lights up during the holiday season. Don't miss a meal aboard the My Old Kentucky Dinner Train.

Visit a Carolina Tree Farm

———◇———

Say what you will about the convenience of an artificial tree, but there's nothing like holiday decorating from the ground up. And there's no better spot to start your hot cider–fueled pursuit of your spindled specimen than at a North Carolina tree farm. The state harvests more than three million trees annually, with Western Carolina—Ashe County, in particular—claiming bragging rights as the state's biggest producer. Ninety-six percent of trees out of North Carolina are Fraser firs, which are native to the Western Appalachian Mountains and beloved for their strong needle retention and sturdy branches. The tree gets its name from John Fraser, a Scottish botanist who explored the Southern Appalachian Mountains of North Carolina in the late 1700s.

Carolina Tree Farms Worth a Visit

MISTLETOE MEADOWS
Laurel Springs

WHY WE LOVE IT
Situated just five miles from the scenic Blue Ridge Parkway, this self-described "farm-to-family" operation run by founder Joe Freeman offers hot cocoa and hayrides in addition to conifers. While Fraser firs are the focus, Mistletoe also grows white pine, blue spruce, and Leyland cypress trees.

DON'T MISS
The farm's other retail lots in Asheboro, Garner, and Pinehurst

LEARN MORE
mistletoe meadows.com

FROSTY'S CHOOSE & CUT
West Jefferson

WHY WE LOVE IT
You can take a hayride or red-trolley ride to find your tree at this sibling-owned farm (a branch of Sexton Farms, just eight miles away), then try your hand at wreath-making and meet Santa himself.

DON'T MISS
The custom souvenir station. After you've found your tree, you can take a slice of the trunk over to a branding station to create a custom souvenir ornament that is stamped with "Frosty's" and the year.

LEARN MORE
gofrostys.com

APPALACHIAN EVERGREENS
Boone

WHY WE LOVE IT
Founded in 1933 by Charles Cole "Charlie" Wilcox, this family farm is now in the hands of his grandson, who goes by the same name.

DON'T MISS
The mail-order options. If you're not lucky enough to visit in person, you can order wreaths, garlands, and tabletop trees. Throw in an order of mountain-cured country ham while you're at it.

LEARN MORE
appevergreens.com

BOYD MOUNTAIN TREE FARM
Waynesville

WHY WE LOVE IT
In the Boyd family for more than 100 years, this 175-acre property has been growing Fraser firs since 1984. Feel free to borrow a bow saw to claim your own.

DON'T MISS
The Boyd family's cabin rentals, which include nine hand-hewn log cabins dating back 150 to 200 years, nestled in a cove overlooking the Smoky Mountains. The property also has three stocked fishing ponds and nature and hiking trails.

LEARN MORE
boydmountain.com

Carolina's Claim to White House Fame

The tradition of placing a Christmas tree in the Blue Room on the State Floor of the White House dates back to President William Howard Taft. However, it was style-setter Jacqueline Kennedy who introduced the idea of giving it a theme when, in 1961, she took inspiration from Tchaikovsky's *The Nutcracker*. Since 1966, members of the National Christmas Tree Association have presented the official White House Christmas Tree for display in the Blue Room, with the grower selected in a national contest after winning their state or regional competitions. Since 1966, North Carolina has sent more trees—which, for the record, must be 18½ feet tall—than any other state.

Go Antiquing for Quilts

FOR THE LOVE OF...
GEE'S BEND QUILTS

For centuries, the women of Gee's Bend, Alabama, have transformed recycled materials like old clothes and feed sacks into extraordinary quilts. These innovative designs come with a history as rich as their patterns. Many quilters are descendants of the Pettway Plantation's enslaved people, making their art a powerful testament to their resilience and creativity. In 2015, three of Gee's Bend's finest—Arlonzia Pettway, Annie Mae Young, and Mary Lee Bendolph (above)—were awarded the National Endowment for the Arts National Heritage Fellowship.

A form of Southern folk art, quilts were born out of necessity. Early quilters, usually women, pieced together humble fabric remnants into beautifully patterned, hand-sewn quilts for use in their own homes or as commemorative works to document a special event. When done communally, this craftsmanship is known as a "quilting bee" and has long been a space for fellowship, celebration, and entrepreneurship. With growing consumer interest in sustainable design, there's a whole new generation seeking out preloved quilts and, during the holiday season, there's a host of ways to embrace them, whether it's repurposing remnants in festive decorative ways (tree skirts, stockings) or gifting a one-of-a-kind heirloom to top beds for years.

HOLIDAY WIT & WISDOM

More ways to jingle as you mingle.

◇

Send a Warm Holiday Card

·····◇·····

CONSIDER YOUR GREETING.
As much as we love
a good "Merry Christmas,"
you may want to
opt for a more inclusive
message like
"Season's Greetings."

INFORM, DON'T BRAG.
Keep it gracious, not
ostentatious. ("We enjoyed
our once-in-a-lifetime
trip" as opposed
to "We were pampered
beyond measure at the
Four Seasons Bora Bora.")

MAKE IT PERSONAL.
A simple message like
"Hope to see you soon,
Abby!" is a nice way for a
mailing to feel intimate.

SKIP THE APOSTROPHE.
Remember: It's
"Happy Holidays
from the Smiths"—not
"the Smith's."

DESIGN WITH A DRAWL

Make a Dolly Tree Topper

"People celebrate me in
their own ways, which I love,"
says singer-songwriter
Dolly Parton. Still, the blonde
beacon of positivity does
have one request: "If you throw
a party in my honor, there
better be some gaud!" Why not
start with the tree, where a
party hat, **glitter paper**, **tinselly
twine**, and a **printout of her
photo** are all you need to create
this kitschy and Christmassy
ode to an Appalachian angel.

Compile a Playlist

These popular tunes
were either
written or performed
by Southerners.

·····◇·····

"Jingle Bells"
Written by
James Pierpont, *Georgia*

**"Have Yourself a
Merry Little Christmas"**
Cowritten by
Hugh Martin, *Alabama*

**"Santa Claus Is
Comin' to Town"**
Cowritten by
Haven Gillespie, *Kentucky*

**"Rockin' Around the
Christmas Tree"**
Performed by
Brenda Lee, *Georgia*

"Pretty Paper"
Written by
Willie Nelson, *Texas*

"Mary, Did You Know?"
Written by
Mark Lowry, *Texas*

Tartan

Fun fact: North Carolina has
the highest percentage of
Scots-Irish ancestry in the
U.S., with South Carolina,
Tennessee, and
West Virginia close behind.

Royal Stewart

Buchanan

Clan Menzies

ONLY IN THE SOUTH...

CHRISTMAS EVE BONFIRES

On December 24th in and around Louisiana's St. James Parish, you'll find as many as 100 pyramid-shaped bonfires (think 20- to 30-feet tall!) set ablaze along the Mississippi River levee to light the way for Papa Noël (aka "Cajun Santa Claus"). The tradition dates back to Southern Louisiana's earliest Cajun settlers and is best enjoyed with bowls of warm gumbo.

HOME REMEDY

Wrangle Your Ribbon

If you're tired of tangled strands littering your wrapping area, organize them with a freestanding paper towel holder. Pull together your most regularly used spools, then stack them on the pole by width—the widest goes on the bottom—to pull and cut with ease.

AROUND THE SOUTH

HOLIDAY HAPPENINGS

There's magic waiting around every corner.

National Gingerbread House Competition
Asheville, North Carolina

In mid-November, all ages convene at the Omni Grove Park Inn to compete for gumdrop glory. The elaborate edible structures remain on display through December.

Lights Spectacular
Johnson City, Texas

Featuring more than 2 million twinkling lights, this Hill Country hamlet an hour west of Austin features a display so dazzling that NASA reported seeing it from space.

The Nutcracker
Birmingham, Alabama

The Alabama Ballet is one of only eight companies in the world licensed by the Balanchine Trust to put on this beloved official production, as it has for 20-plus years.

Dickens of a Christmas
Franklin, Tennessee

The historic downtown transforms into a Victorian village filled with food, music, arts-and-crafts vendors, and ye olde celebrity sightings. (Ebeneezer Scrooge! Tiny Tim!)

Irish National

Clan MacGregor

Clan MacKinnon

Index

Credits

All illustrations by
Melinda Josie
Buff Strickland 1
Max Kim-Bee 2–3
Becky Luigart-Stayner 5, 25, 26, 35, 36, 39, 41, 45, 50, 56, 73, 75, 78, 79, 99, 103, 104, 118, 119, 121, 127, 129, 132, 143, 145, 154, 158, 166, 167, 170–171, 172, 173, 180, 181, 186, 188, 197, 202, 205, 206, 214, 215
Mary Britton Senseney 6
Brian Woodcock 9, 17, 19, 26, 28–32, 46, 49, 58–59, 71, 78, 100, 111, 119, 123, 126, 130, 132, 134–140, 149, 150, 161, 172, 182, 188, 189, 190–194, 201, 217
Jackie Greaney 9, 89, 111
Monica Buck 9, 179, 215
Dimitrije Tanaskovic/Stocksy United 10–11
Brent Darby Photography 12
Deborah Arends/ @Addictedtochina 12
Getty Images 12, 62–63, 64, 118, 163, 165, 212
Daniel Cedergren 12
Adam Ford, Interior Design by A.A. Ford Interiors 13
David Tsay 13, 23, 73, 124
Laurey W. Glenn 15 Styling by Lizzie Cox 19
Alison Gootee 18, 78
Courtesy of Jenny Wolf Interiors 19
Annie Schlechter 21, 132, 172, 175, 181, 182
Philip Friedman/Studio D 27
Mali Azima 38
Ian Palmer. Food Styling by Torie Cox 42, 157, 198
Jillian Savage 53

Clarissa Burgess 54
Anna Dean 55
Jeff Wilson 55
Jack Thompson 55
John Davidson 55
Jeffrey Greenberg/Universal Images Group via Getty Images 56
Ali Harper 64
Raymond Forbes LLC/ Stocksy United 65
Rikki Snyder 65, 173
Dana Gallagher 67, 70, 124
Roger Davies 69, 73
David Hillegas 70, 71, 78, 110
Julie Soefer 71
Brie Williams 72, 125, 127
Mirrorpix via Getty Images 72
CBS via Getty Images 72
Pictorial Press Ltd/Alamy Stock Photo 72
Helen Norman 76, 116–117, 118, 124
Tara Donne 80–86
Susan Kaufman 90
Ren Fuller 93, 96, 146
Anna Kern 95
Leslee Mitchell 107
Alicia Osborne Photography 108, 109
Getty Images/iStockphoto 109
Lee Bray 109
Jessica Sample 109
Jean Allsopp 113, 185
Alyssa Lee 124
Lincoln Barbour 127
Michael Partenio 133
Hector M. Sanchez 153
Maggie Braucher 162, 163
Brookings Fly Shop 163
Courtesy of Old Edwards Inn 163
Courtesy of Oklahoma State Fair 164
Emily Followill 177
Burcu Avsar 178, 179, 188
David A. Land 179, 182, 209
Lisa Flood 179

Lucas Allen 181
Dylan Chandler 182
Rett Peek 183
Courtesy of Jenny Bohannon 188
Courtesy of Jay Hubbard/ The Middleburg Eccentric 210
Jodi & Kurt Photography 211
Ron Sachs/CNP/Alamy Stock Photo 211
Rachel Clarke 211
Katie Urban 211
Chip Somodevilla/Getty Images 213

Special thanks to the many talented designers and homeowners whose projects and homes are featured throughout the book, including:

Jenny Bohannon, Melissa & David Bowen, Jenni Bowlin, Kelley Brown Interiors, Kaley Cutting, Bambi Costanzo, Elizabeth Demos, The Design Atelier, Dodson Interiors, Megan Duncan, Meredith Ellis, James Farmer, The Farmhouse Project, A.A. Ford Interiors, Lisa Flood, Shelia Frey, Christina Gore, Lori Guyer, Heather Chadduck Hillegas, Trinity Holmes, Debra Koehler, Richard Keith Langham, Lucy Interiors, Bailey McCarthy, Becca McDowell, Whitney McGregor, Patrick McGuire, Hillary Munro, Nora Murphy, Lauren Northup, O'Hara Interiors, Pfeffer Torode, Heather Taylor, Ronnie Thompson, Lea Ann Walker, Jenny Wolf, Amy Whyte, Holly Audrey Williams, Rachel Wright, Claire Zinnecker

CountryLiving

EDITOR-IN-CHIEF: Rachel Hardage Barrett
DESIGN DIRECTOR: Maribeth Jones **MANAGING EDITOR:** Amy Lowe Mitchell
VISUAL DIRECTOR: Kate Phillips **VISUAL EDITOR:** Ian Palmer
FOOD AND CRAFTS DIRECTOR: Charlyne Mattox
COPY EDITOR: Stephanie Gibson Lepore

HEARST HOME
VICE PRESIDENT, PUBLISHER: Jacqueline Deval
DEPUTY DIRECTOR: Nicole Fisher
DEPUTY MANAGING EDITOR: Maria Ramroop
SENIOR PHOTO EDITOR: Cinzia Reale-Castello

CO-AUTHOR: Jeanne Lyons Davis
PROJECT EDITOR: Leah Tracosas Jenness
INTERIOR ART DIRECTOR: Erynn Hassinger **COVER ART DIRECTOR:** Matt Ryan
DIGITAL IMAGE SPECIALIST: Ruth Vazquez
COPY EDITOR: Gabrielle Danchick

PUBLISHED BY HEARST
PRESIDENT & CHIEF EXECUTIVE OFFICER: Steven R. Swartz
CHAIRMAN: William R. Hearst III
EXECUTIVE VICE CHAIRMAN: Frank A. Bennack, Jr.

HEARST MAGAZINE MEDIA, INC
PRESIDENT: Debi Chirichella
GENERAL MANAGER, HEARST LIFESTYLE GROUP: Ronak Patel
GLOBAL CHIEF REVENUE OFFICER: Lisa Ryan Howard
EDITORIAL DIRECTOR: Lucy Kaylin
CHIEF FINANCIAL & STRATEGY OFFICER; TREASURER: Regina Buckley
CONSUMER GROWTH OFFICER: Lindsey Horrigan
CHIEF PRODUCT & TECHNOLOGY OFFICER: Daniel Bernard
PRESIDENT, HEARST MAGAZINES INTERNATIONAL: Jonathan Wright
SECRETARY: Catherine A. Bostron
PUBLISHING CONSULTANTS: Gilbert C. Maurer, Mark F. Miller

Library of Congress Cataloging-in-Publication Data available on request

10 9 8 7 6 5 4 3 2 1

Published by Hearst Home, an imprint of Hearst Books/
Hearst Communications, Inc. 300 W 57th Street New York, NY 10019

Country Living is a registered trademark of Hearst Magazine Media, Inc.
and Hearst Home, the Hearst Home logo, and Hearst Books are
registered trademarks of Hearst Communications, Inc.

For information about custom editions, special sales, premium
and corporate purchases: hearst.com/magazines/hearst-books

Printed in China

978-1-958395-76-9